JESUS
THE
MEEK KING

JESUS THE MEEK KING

DEIRDRE J. GOOD

TRINITY PRESS INTERNATIONAL
Harrisburg, Pennsylvania

Trinity Press International, P.O. Box 1321, Harrisburg, PA 17105
Trinity Press International is a division of the Morehouse Group.

Cover design: Al Cetta

Cover art:
Giotto di Bondone (1266–1336). *Entry of Christ into Jerusalem.*
Scrovegni Chapel, Padua, Italy. Alinari/Art Resource, New York.

Library of Congress Cataloging-in-Publication Data
Good, Deirdre Joy.
    Jesus the meek king / Deirdre J. Good.
       p. cm.
    Includes bibliographical references (p.   ) and index.
    ISBN 1-56338-284-9 (pa. : alk paper)
    1. Jesus Christ – Royal office – History of doctrines. 2. Meekness –
History. 3. Praos (The Greek word)   I. Title.
BT270.G66 1999
225.4'87–dc21   99-27565

Printed in the United States of America

99 00 01 02 03 04   10 9 8 7 6 5 4 3 2 1

For Frank
(1953–1996)
and Julian

CONTENTS

ACKNOWLEDGMENTS

I would like to thank people without whom this book would not have assumed its present shape. My colleagues David Green, Dick Corney, Celia Deutsch, Amy-Jill Levine, and Mark Kiley all read and commented on various drafts of the chapters. Their advice was immensely helpful, and I took much of it.

The board of trustees of The General Theological Seminary granted me two sabbaticals in the last six years during the course of which I spent some time thinking about the subject matter of the book. The Conant fund of the Board for Theological Education enabled me to spend one of the two sabbaticals at Union Theological Seminary, where I used the reading room of the Burke Library with profit. Many people listened and made helpful comments while I shared early drafts of different chapters at Christian education forums in parishes in and around New York City. Students at GTS listened and commented on various parts of the book. However, I alone am responsible for its final form, warts and all.

I would like to thank Tom Ferrante at St. Mark's Library of The General Theological Seminary; he obtained books for me on interlibrary loan at short notice.

My thanks also to Hal Rast of TPI for accepting the book for publication. Al Cetta has my gratitude for the beautiful cover.

Certain circumstances combined to bring the book into being. My colon cancer diagnosis caused a hiatus from writing, and when the chemotherapy was over, an enormous desire to finish the book. I hope it is the better for such an experience. I know adversity has given me less patience for certain things and more gratitude for others. *Non quid sed quemadmodum feras interest.*

ABBREVIATIONS

'Abot R. Nat.	*'Abot de Rabbi Nathan*
11QT	Temple Scroll
1Q, 4Q	Numbered caves of Qumran, scrolls from; followed by abbreviation or number of document
1QS	*Rule of the Community, Manual of Discipline* (Qumran)
4Q171	Pesher on Psalms from Qumran Cave 4
4QDa	Daniel from Qumran Cave 4
Ad. Nic.	Isocrates *Ad Nicoclem* (*To Nicocles*)
Ant.	Josephus *Antiquities of the Jews*
AV	Authorized Version (King James Version)
b. *'Abot*	*'Abot* (Babylonian Talmud)
b. *Sanh.*	*Sanhedrin* (Babylonian Talmud)
Contra Ap.	Josephus *Contra Apion*
De coh. ira	Plutarch *De cohibenda ira* (*On the Control of Anger*)
De frat. amor.	Plutarch *De fraterno amore* (*On Brotherly Love*)
De Ira	Seneca *On Anger*
De Jos.	Philo *De Josepho* (*On Joseph*)
De virt. et vitio	Plutarch *De virtute et vitio* (*Virtue and Vice*)
De virt. morali	Plutarch *De virtute morali* (*On Moral Virtue*)
Did.	*Didache*
Ep. Arist.	*Epistle of Aristeas*
ET	English translation
Eth. Nic.	Aristotle *Ethica Nicomachea* (*Nicomachean Ethics*)

Herm. Man.	*Shepherd of Hermas Mandates*
Hist. eccl.	Eusebius *Historia ecclesiastica* (*Ecclesiastical History*)
Ign. Eph.	Ignatius *Letter to the Ephesians*
Ign. Pol.	Ignatius *Letter to Polycarp*
Ign. Trall.	Ignatius *Letter to the Trallians*
J. W.	Josephus *Jewish Wars*
Leg. ad Gaium	Philo *Legatio ad Gaium*
LXX	Septuagint
Men.	Plato *Meno*
Nat. Fac.	Galen *Peri physikōn dynameōn* (*On Natural Faculties*)
NEB	New English Bible
Ned.	*Nedarim*
NSRV	New Revised Standard Version
Od.	Homer *Odyssey*
PG	*Patrologiae Graeca*, ed. J.-P. Migne
PL	*Patrologia Latina*, ed. J.-P. Migne
P. Oxy.	*Oxyrhynchus Papyri*, ed. B. P. Grendell and A. S. Hunt (1898–)
Paneg.	Isocrates *Panegyricus*
Phd.	Plato *Phaedo*
Pol.	Aristotle *Politics*
Rh.	Aristotle *Rhetoric*
RSV	Revised Standard Version
Shab.	*Shabbat*
Sipre Num.	*Sipre* Numbers
t. *Sot.*	*Sota* (Tosephta)
y. *Sot.*	*Sota* (Jerusalem Talmud)

INTRODUCTION

Jesus proclaimed God's kingdom, and he was killed as a would-be king. His disciples expected the kingdom to return after Jesus' death.[1] But what does it mean to describe Jesus as a *praus* king (Matt. 21:5)? Jesus calls himself *praus* in Matthew 11:29 ("for I am *praus* and humble of heart"). What does it mean to describe Moses in the same way in the Greek translation of the Hebrew Scriptures ("and the person Moses was very *praus*" [Num. 12:3])? Traditionally *praus* has been translated as "meek." Contemporary translations, however, are more likely to use the word "gentle" or "humble." How does this clarify the bearing of a king? What does it mean to call Jesus or Moses *praus*? And what sort of king was Jesus?

To describe someone as "meek" or a group of people as "humble" is to speak about the quality of their character and their behavior. It is to attach value to some aspect of who they are or what they do. Attaching value to an action implies a positive assessment of the purpose of that action. When we call someone gentle or brave or good, we are evaluating that person against a standard. We are, moreover, using a word that seems comprehensible. We all know, do we not, what it means to be gentle or brave or good? Descriptions of personal moral qualities seem to have a timeless character. And so we take it for granted that our understanding of these concepts is one that is common to humankind throughout its history, unchanged by historical circumstances. Were we to say that "Jesus was a first-century Jew," we would recognize that we are making a historical statement. To understand its import, we would need to know something about the Judaisms of the first century. If, however, we say "Jesus was humble," we are not making a historical statement. To call Moses "meek" does

1. E. P. Sanders, *Jesus and Judaism* (Philadelphia: Fortress, 1985), 307. Sanders asserts in a discussion of the triumphal entry (306) that the disciples knew that Jesus "was to be a special kind of king." What does this mean?

1

not fix him at a particular time or place. The same concept carries different connotations for ancient and modern readers,[2] and
it is necessary to investigate changes of meaning in descriptions of
moral qualities, not just because there are such changes but also
because the apparently abstract character of these adjectives mask
such changes behind the illusion of similarity.

Unwary modern readers who do not pay attention to these distinctions in the meaning of values between ancient and modern
times might think that the same word carries the same freight in
two different contexts. This seems to be the premise of several of
William J. Bennett's publications since *The Book of Virtues*.[3] While
we recognize that words like "family" are construed differently in
different times, we need to observe that even labels of virtues are
particular to time and place. To understand what they might con-
note we need to pay attention to the words themselves and the
context in which they occur.

Readers for whom the biblical text has either interest or authority would naturally find a Greek word describing Moses and
Jesus to be of sufficient interest to warrant further study. At this
time, however, we are on a semantic cusp that gives this study
some urgency. The stability of rendering the Greek *praus* by the
English word "meek" is being undermined. From William Tyndale until recently, the English word "meek" has carried almost
all of the connotations of the Greek word *praus*. Now the English
word "meek" has taken on connotations severing it from its older
meanings. In the *Oxford English Dictionary*, the meaning "gentle,
courteous, kind" is marked as obsolete. Current usage gives the
term unfavorable connotations. It sometimes describes those likely
to submit tamely to oppression or injury.[4] The *New York Times*
crossword puzzle for July 17, 1996, gave the clue "undemanding"
for the solution "meek." Only a particular kind of leader would
use the word. Vaclav Havel includes it in a discussion of human
characteristics: "For this reason [consciousness precedes being], the
salvation of this human world lies nowhere else than in the human

---

2. Handbooks and dictionaries of biblical social values exist to clarify differ-
ences. See John J. Pilch and Bruce J. Malina, eds., *Biblical Social Values and Their
Meanings: A Handbook* (Peabody, Mass.: Hendrickson, 1993).
    3. William J. Bennett, *The Book of Virtues: A Treasury of Great Moral Stories*
(New York: Simon and Schuster, 1993); *The Moral Compass: Stories for a Life's
Journey* (New York: Simon and Schuster, 1995); *The Children's Book of Heroes*
(New York: Simon and Schuster, 1997).
    4. *Oxford English Dictionary (Second Edition) on Compact Disc* (Oxford:
Oxford University Press, 1992), s.v. "meek."

heart, in the human power to reflect, in human meekness and in human responsibility."[5]

This current understanding of "meek" reverberates in modern translations of the Bible, where the word "meek" is often replaced by the word "gentle" or "humble." The New English Bible (NEB) has done the most to accelerate this trend. Where the Authorized Version (AV) translated the Hebrew of Numbers 12:3 as "(Now the man Moses *was* very meek, above all the men which *were* upon the face of the earth.)"[6] the NEB translates it as "Moses was in fact a man of great humility, the most humble man on earth." The NEB and its successor, the Revised English Bible (REB), speak of Jesus as "gentle and humble-hearted" at Matthew 11:29 and as coming "in gentleness" at 21:5. Where the AV reads "blessed are the meek" at Matthew 5:5, the NEB translates "how blest are those of a gentle spirit." In Matthew 11:29 and 21:5, the New Revised Standard Version (NRSV) describes Jesus as "gentle" or "humble." However, the NRSV retains the term "meek" when it is used as a collective noun in the Psalms and in Matthew 5:5.

Thus, if we read only the NEB or the REB, the word "meek" would have disappeared. If we read the NRSV, we would find the older word used in some places but replaced in others. Why did the translators of this influential and widely used version think the English term "meek" inapplicable to a male leader but applicable to a community? Are the opening words of the Sermon on the Mount in Matthew's Gospel as stable as the English version of the Lord's Prayer in the same Gospel? Does "gentle" or "humble" adequately convey the nuances of the Hebrew or Greek words that had been translated as "meek"? Such questions deserve exploration.

When we speak of values, we must not confuse the word with the reality. If we are interested in words, then the most important tool is the lexicon. But if we are interested in ideas, then it is not useful to study words alone. We need to look at the immediate and the wider context. We also need to consider that the idea a word conveys may be discussed without that word being present in a text.

---

5. "The Revolution Has Just Begun," *Time*, March 5, 1990, 14–15, on Vaclav Havel. The recent edition of Havel's speeches by Paul Wilson, *The Art of the Impossible* (New York: Knopf, 1997) translates the same passage as "human modesty" (18).

6. The parentheses are a decision made by the English translators. The words in italics are not found in the Hebrew text.

The Greek word *praus* itself has a long history. In the beginning *praos* (its earlier form) described qualities suitable for those
in subordinate positions. In the Homeric period women were commended for quiet virtues such as meekness and qualities such as
beauty, skill in weaving and housekeeping, chastity, and faithfulness. When the shade of Agamemnon says that Penelope is "full of
virtue" and that "the fame of her virtue shall never perish," he is
commending her for her faithful and loyal behavior toward her
husband, Odysseus.[7] In contrast, commendable qualities of men
appear in contexts of public excellence and competition. Homeric society values in men qualities it deems essential to security and
stability. Excellence is not inherent. It is men of nobility who determine the nature of excellence for both men and women; a woman
within the Homeric household has no need of competitive excellence. The same word, "excellence" or "virtue," may be used to
convey differing qualities in men on the one hand and in women
or slaves on the other.[8]

Somewhat later, the philosophers Plato and Aristotle reverse
Homeric understanding and commend the practice of cooperative
virtues.[9] Societal goals have altered: value is now attached to the
prosperity and stability of the state. And yet successful manage-
ment is not enough in itself. To the ability to administer a city
(for an Athenian man) or a household (for an Athenian woman)
must now be added the qualities of justice and temperance.[10] Adversity, argues Plato, such as the loss of wealth or a comrade at
arms, is to be borne meekly and without fuss. In the Homeric period defeat in battle would have been a matter of great shame and
loss of honor, for it could mean being taken into slavery. Plato
endeavors to show that the apparent failure of Socrates' life, his
imprisonment and ignominious death, was in fact an expression of
his qualities. Probably the most famous Athenian, he is the noblest,
most gentle (*praotaton*), and best man, according to those witness-
ing his death.[11] Generally, a person acting meekly is not upset by
other people or circumstances. While some women (and bad men)

---

7. Homer *Od.* 24.193.
8. Arthur Adkins, *Merit and Responsibility: A Study in Greek Values* (Oxford:
Clarendon, 1960), 36–37. In the present discussion I am using the terms "virtue"
and "excellence" interchangeably to reflect the Greek word *aretē*.
9. Aristotle *Rh.* 1366B.
10. Plato *Men.* 73A 6–9.
11. Plato *Phd.* 116C.

may lament publicly, emotions are not expressed by any virtuous person.[12]

Later, in the Hellenistic world, leaders are called *praos*. Religious pioneers, statesmen, politicians, and governors either commend themselves as meek or receive this accolade from others. As the philosopher Isocrates and the historian Josephus show, demonstrating compassion toward the less fortunate indicates that a *praos* man is likely to belong to the nobility. What distinguishes the descriptions of *praotēs* in Hellenistic writers from those in Plato is their signal interest in its acquisition. If latent, *praotēs* must be realized. If absent, it must be taught. Thus philosophers dispense advice to young rulers advocating not tyranny but compassion toward citizens in their care. To be *praos* is to be compassionate and kind: "Do nothing in anger. . . . Show yourself stern by overlooking nothing that happens, but *praos* by making the punishment less than the offense," Isocrates counsels the young king of Cyprus shortly after 374 B.C.E.[13] Self-awareness leads to self-discipline. Nicocles governs himself and thus can govern others.

In the eyes of the first-century Jewish historian Josephus, the emperor Titus displays magnanimity in his conduct during the siege of Jerusalem in the war against Rome (66–70 C.E.). "Throw down your arms," Titus implores the Jewish leaders. "Surrender your persons, and I grant you your lives, like a *praos* master of a household punishing the incorrigible and preserving the rest for myself."[14] At the point of his conquest over Jerusalem the emperor Titus acts in the manner of a Hellenistic ruler. To those facing defeat he is benevolent, not tyrannical.

For readers of the Greek translation of the Hebrew Scriptures in the same period, the description of Moses as "very *praus*, more so than anyone else on earth"[15] would give to Moses traits of Hellenistic leadership. The first-century Jewish writer Philo describes this aspect of Moses' character as king and high priest in his two books on Moses. Well after the first century, Moses' meekness was a virtue to be imitated: "The Holy One, blessed be He, causes his divine presence to rest only on him who is strong, wealthy, wise, and meek; and all these are deduced from Moses."[16] Rabbi Hillel's proverbial gentleness may have been emphasized precisely because

---

12. Plato *Republic* 387E.
13. Isocrates *Ad. Nic.* 23.
14. Josephus *J. W.* 6.350.
15. Numbers 12:3 (LXX).
16. *Ned.* 38a.

it was Mosaic: "Our Rabbis taught: A man should always be gentle like Hillel and not impatient like Shammai."[17]

In the Greek translation of the Psalms, we find the Israelite community called "the meek": "The Lord lifts up the *praeis:* he casts the wicked to the ground."[18] The word *praeis* translates the Hebrew plural *anawim.* In this body of literature the noun portrays a class of disadvantaged people on behalf of whom God acts. There is a sense of reciprocity to the term: they can be meek because God acts on their behalf.

Appropriating the language of the Psalms, the community of the Dead Sea Scrolls understood itself to be "the congregation of the poor (*anawim*)."[19] One text draws a comparison between the role of a slave serving the master and that of a community member performing and delighting in the will of God and his commands. The individual lives out the moral code by which the community lives and is taught how to answer the haughty in meekness.[20] Elsewhere *anawah* is part of a list of dispositional virtues that shape social behavior.[21] This suggests the subordination of individual interests to the well-being of the community. It also defines the community's self-understanding over and against outsiders.

Appropriating this same language from Psalms to a Greek-speaking milieu, the first-century community behind Matthew's Gospel calls itself "the *praeis*" and "the poor in spirit."[22] Community instructions include mutual forgiveness and restoration of a repentant member.[23] Other early Christian communities, like the communities of the Dead Sea Scrolls and that of Matthew's Gospel, esteem certain qualities for the promotion and enhancement of common life. By emphasizing gentle qualities — obedience, humility, meekness, patience, long-suffering, endurance — some Christian groups begin to commend virtues previously connected with women and slaves. How this commendation affects the social status of women and slaves is a subject for further study.

In Matthew's Gospel, Jesus invites listeners to heed instruction

---

17. *Shab.* 30b–31a; *Sipre* Num. 101; *'Abot R. Nat.* A15; t. *Sot.* 13:3; b. *Sanh.* 11a. Cited in Dale C. Allison, *The New Moses: A Matthean Typology* (Minneapolis: Fortress, 1993), 71–72.

18. Psalm 146:6 (LXX) = Psalm 147:6 (ET); see also Psalm 24:9 (LXX) = Psalm 25:9 (ET) and Psalm 36:11 (LXX) = Psalm 37:11 (ET) and elsewhere.

19. The scrolls are written in Hebrew or Aramaic.

20. 1QS 11,1.

21. 1QS 2,24; 4,3.

22. Matthew 5:3, 5.

23. Matthew 18:15–22.

on the basis of his meekness: "Take my yoke upon you, and learn from me; for I am *praus* and lowly of heart."[24] In the wider context of the Hellenistic world, Matthew seems to set Jesus alongside other rulers. This interpretation of Matthew is confirmed by a version of the same passage in the *Gospel of Thomas,* which includes the word "lordship": "Come unto me: for my yoke is easy and my lordship is meek, and you will find repose for yourselves."[25] Yet Matthew 11:28 has suggested to some that meekness and lowliness define each other without any leadership connotations.[26]

Other writers in religious traditions use the meekness of great men as the basis of their exhortation. In the first century, the Jewish writer Paul pleads in a letter to people he knew at Corinth: "I myself, Paul, appeal to you by the *prautēs* and gentleness of Christ."[27] While he does discuss meekness as a quality, he connects it to aspects of his own leadership among the Corinthians. Its meaning is not far from the notion of disciplined calmness found in Hellenistic texts.

In the Matthean and in some Pauline communities we see juxtaposed the community's self-description and the picture of an individual displaying the same traits. Paul appeals to the meekness of Christ in 2 Corinthians 10:1. At 1 Corinthians 4:14–21 he discusses the nature of his leadership: he exercises love and compassion rather than tyranny. Paul asks the Corinthians if they wish him to visit them "with a rod or in love and with a spirit of meekness (*prautetos*)." Whether citing the example of Christ or a model of leadership known to his own Hellenistic audience, Paul's appeal is to the familiar. In the Matthean community, it is by attending to the model of a meek Jesus that a reader discovers how to practice disciplined calmness. Here, the leader's conduct in the narrative of

---

24. Matthew 11:29.
25. *Gospel of Thomas* saying 90. Marvin Meyer, ed. and trans., *The Gospel of Thomas* (San Francisco: HarperSanFrancisco, 1992), 59, translates: "Jesus said: Come to me, for my yoke is easy and my mastery is gentle, and you will find rest for yourselves."
26. Daniel Patte, *The Gospel according to Matthew: A Structural Commentary on Matthew's Faith* (Philadelphia: Fortress, 1987; Valley Forge, Pa.: Trinity Press International, 1996), 164–65, sees the description of Jesus as meek and lowly in heart as identifying him with the "babes" to whom revelation is given in 11:27. "Since the 'babes' to whom 'these things' are revealed is contrasted with the wise or intelligent, they are simply defined in the text as the people who have no such pretension. They are 'poor in spirit' (5:3), 'lowly in heart' or humble (see 11:29) by contrast with the Israelite cities that presume to have a privileged relationship with God."
27. 2 Corinthians 10:1.

the text shapes and supports the quiet virtues enhancing common life. What Jesus says and does models the behavior of the community. Other texts from the period of Christian origins can commend community virtues without recourse to a leadership model.[28]

Some later commentaries understood meekness to be present in the biblical text by implication in passages where the term itself was not found. In the tenth century, the great Jewish scholar Rashi describes the patriarch Abraham's answer to God in Genesis 22: " 'Here I am.' Such is the answer of the pious: it is an expression of meekness (*anawah*) and readiness."[29] This example serves to remind the reader that investigations of words or ideas cannot be restricted to places where they are explicit.

Christian commentators have tended to sit uncomfortably with notions of passivity in descriptions of the meek as an oppressed and disenfranchised group whose lowly status God will advance. For example, the early twentieth-century Anglican bishop Charles Gore said that the meek of Matthew 5:5 are "those ready to be put upon" to whom God says, "Friend, come up higher!"[30] Bishop Gore's unease with passivity leads him to read a more active meaning in Matthew 5:5.

This brief historical survey raises certain questions. Why is the christological model of disciplined calmness absent from modern discussions of meekness in biblical texts? Why are the gender implications of the term not explored in modern commentaries? Why has the older idea of disciplined calmness and a rejection of force dropped from contemporary use of the word "meek"?

The value of the present study is twofold. It will enable readers to balance societal expectations of self-realization and individuation with community values, and it will contribute to the present discussion of gender construction and issues of leadership and power. The first chapter discusses the linguistic issues and the approach of the present study. It takes the study of the word as a paradigm. Chapter 2 discusses dispositional qualities like meekness. *Praotēs* appears in the context of the notion of brotherhood in Hellenistic texts, including Plutarch and the New Testament. Chapter 3 explores the Hellenistic idea of kingship. Chapter 4 discusses moral values in Matthew's Gospel, with particular attention

---

28. James.

29. M. Rosenbaum and A. M. Silbermann, eds., *Pentateuch with Targum Onkelos, Haphtaroth and Rashi's Commentary*, 5 vols. (London: Shapiro, Vallentine, 1929–34), 1:93.

30. Charles Gore, *The Sermon on the Mount* (London: John Murray, 1896), 35.

to the model of a meek king. Chapter 5 investigates use of "the meek" as a self-description by Jewish and Christian communities as part of the emerging vocabulary of subservience and how the term functions to enhance community life. Using Jewish and Christian texts, particularly those from the western Christian monastic tradition, it also explores the idea of humility and power. An epilogue discusses briefly the rich history of the English word "meek" in translations of the Bible from Tyndale to the present day.

Chapter 1

WORDS, DICTIONARIES, AND TEXTS

In Hellenistic literature including the Septuagint, the Greek root under discussion may occur in different forms: as the adjective *praus*[1] ("Behold, your king is coming to you, *meek,* and mounted on an ass");[2] as the noun *prautēs*[3] ("Therefore rid yourselves of all sordidness and rank growth of wickedness and welcome with *meekness* the implanted word which is able to save your souls";[4] and as the verb *praunō* ("Philosophy...has educated us for public affairs and *made us meek* toward each other").[5] The adjective may occur in the plural form *praeis* ("But *the meek* shall possess the land and delight themselves in abundant prosperity").[6] There is also an adverb, *praos* ("Macro admonished Gaius *meekly* and quietly").[7] In Hellenistic and early Christian literature, all these forms are found. In the New Testament, the verb never occurs. The noun is found almost exclusively in the Epistles of the New Testament. The adjective occurs in both the Gospels and the Epistles.

Using Dictionaries

To understand the Greek term *praus,* one could use a dictionary where there is customarily a one-word equivalent. Linguists call

---

1. The form *praos* also occurs in 2 Maccabees 15:12; Josephus *Contra Ap.* 1.267; and frequently in Philo.
2. Matthew 21:5.
3. The earlier form, *praotēs,* occurs in Plato, Aristotle, Isocrates, the letters of Ignatius, *Shepherd of Hermas Mandates,* and Plutarch.
4. James 1:21.
5. Isocrates *Paneg.* 47. Since the English verb "to meeken" is obsolete, I have translated "made meek."
6. Psalm 37:11.
7. Philo *Leg. ad Gaium* 7.43.

this a gloss, since it substitutes one word for another. As an illustration, I take Matthew 21:5. A standard Greek lexicon for the New Testament defines the adjective as "gentle, humble, considerate, meek in the older favorable sense," and for Matthew 21:5, "unassuming."[8] The same lexicon defines the noun *prautēs* as "gentleness, humility, courtesy, considerateness, meekness in the older favorable sense" and connects it with *epieikeia* and other qualities and virtues.[9] Although it does cite passages where the word occurs, the flaw in this approach is that it cannot consider all the relevant contexts. Context supplies meaning. A reader, failing to find a more specific definition, would be encouraged to transfer the general meaning of the adjective to Matthew 21:5. An "unassuming" king rides into Jerusalem. "Unassuming" might describe the demeanor of a modest man, but if it describes that of a king it surely needs explanation. The lexicon leaves more questions than it answers.

How might we understand the wider connotations of "meekness" by using lexicons? We could consult a lexicon that places the word within an environment of words with similar meaning. One such Greek lexicon, which is based on semantic domains, locates *praus* within the semantic domain of moral and ethical qualities and related behavior.[10] Here we find a presentation of the word in both an immediate environment and a wider environment. The benefit of such a lexicon is that authors often use words with more than one meaning. At the same time, they do not usually imply the entire semantic domain for the word every time it is used. The word itself does that. Context, however, furnishes one way of interpreting a word. Broader context or intratextual use of a word may move the discussion of meaning toward other areas of interpretation.

What is the semantic domain of *praus?* In the immediate environment, the general purport of *prautēs* is given rather than a one-word definition ("gentleness of attitude and behavior, in con-

---

8. Walter Bauer, William F. Arndt, F. Wilbur Gingrich, and Frederick W. Danker, eds., *A Greek-English Lexicon of the New Testament and Other Early Christian Literature* (Chicago: University of Chicago Press, 1979), 698–99.
9. Ibid., 699.
10. Johannes P. Louw and Eugene A. Nida, eds., *Greek-English Lexicon of the New Testament Based on Semantic Domains*, 2 vols. (New York: United Bible Societies, 1988), 1:742. Our word is under "Gentleness, Mildness," 88.59–88.65. A semantic domain (sometimes called a synonym set) brings together closely related meanings often regarded as partial synonyms and different, especially opposite meanings (antonyms).

trast with harshness in one's dealings with others — 'gentleness, meekness, mildness' "), and is associated with *praus* ("pertaining to being gentle and mild — 'mild, gentle, meek' "), *ēpios* ("pertaining to being gentle with the implication of kindness — 'gentle, kind' "), *epieikeia* ("the quality of gracious forbearing — 'gentleness, graciousness, forbearance' "), *epieikēs* ("pertaining to being gracious and forbearing — 'gentle, gracious, forbearing' "), *tapeinos* ("pertaining to being meek, with the implication of low status — 'gentle, meek, and mild' "), and *metriopatheō* ("to be gentle in one's attitude toward someone — 'to deal gently with, to be gently disposed toward' ").[11] The lexicon's wider domain of moral and ethical qualities in which the subdomain *prautēs* is located has twenty-six subdomains, each with several words, as well as twelve other subdomains containing negative qualities. To move away from the simple one-word substitution of the first lexicon and toward a definition of the word is an advantage.[12] By placing *prautēs* in a context of words relating to moral and ethical qualities we see it within the broader framework. The size of the domain in which *praus* falls suggests an enormous interest in the topic of the domain on the part of New Testament writers.

However, the means for taking context into account still falls short for Matthew 21:5. The lexicon encourages a translation of *praus* by "mild, gentle, or meek," and the paragraph heading is "gentleness, mildness." But the context of the word *praus* in Matthew 21:5 is that of kingship. By using the word in a context of kingship, the semantic domain is qualified. To explain the particular connotation of *praus* in the context of kingship we must look elsewhere. There are discussions of moral qualities of persons in authority in Greek literature of the time. For example, the Greek Additions to Esther, dated to the first century B.C.E., contain a letter of the great king, Artaxerxes, who writes to governors from India to Ethiopia:

> Having become ruler of many nations and master of the whole world (not elated with presumption of authority but always acting reasonably and with *kindness*[13]) I have determined to settle the lives of my subjects....[14]

---

11. Ibid., 749.
12. Ibid., vii.
13. The Greek word is a form of *ēpios*, a term that both dictionaries discussed above associate closely with *praus*.
14. Additions to Esther 13:2 (LXX following 3:13).

In another part of the same text, Esther, having prayed to God, goes to meet the king to whom she speaks for her people. The king reacts:

> Lifting his face, flushed with splendor, he looked at her in fierce anger. The queen faltered and turned pale and faint... then God changed the spirit of the king to *prautēs,* and in alarm he sprang from his throne and took her in his arms until she came to herself.[15]

These two passages combine kingship with the moral qualities of kindness and gentleness. They clarify the demeanor of a meek Hellenistic ruler: compassionate forbearance for subjects rather than despotism or anger. Although the two words overlap in meaning, they are not synonyms. The context for the exercise of the king's gentleness in the latter passage is a transformation of spirit (by an external agency) from fury to compassion. Only the context reveals a contrast of anger and meekness. From these two passages we can see that meekness is like gentleness insofar as it is a moral quality connoting kindness. It is exercised by men in power. It is the quality of a benevolent rather than a tyrannical king. But meekness also involves the overcoming of anger.[16] This does not seem to be the case with *ēpios*. This context of the benevolent exercise of royal power appears to be the appropriate context for interpreting Matthew 21:5. Of course, to avoid the charge of transferring a meaning from one passage to another we will have to investigate this thesis in the context of the Gospel. This I will shortly do.

To find our root in this particular context, one can do a Boolean search of Greek databases under the words for "king" (or royal qualities like "authority" or "power") and "gentleness" or "kindness." I found the texts from Esther in the Septuagint by using the program BibleWorks.[17] Using a concordance would take longer because regardless of cross-references every word must be looked up separately, but this process would produce the same result.

Locating a word in a semantic domain creates a broader semantic framework than is found in a typical dictionary. Out of this framework meaning comes through the observation of similarity, distinction, and opposition. As we have seen, "meekness" probably differs from *ēpios* in that meekness connotes a disciplined rejection

---

15. Additions to Esther 15:7–8 (LXX following 5:1–2).
16. See further discussion in chapters 4 and 5.
17. BibleWorks for Windows 3.5 (Big Fork, Mont.: Hermeneutika, 1996).

of anger on the part of a man in a position of power. "Anger" is one of the negative subdomains of moral and ethical qualities, and "meekness" is understood in opposition to it.[18] Thus the reader is prepared for that rejection of anger by a meek king encountered within the immediate context of the root "meek" in Matthew and the Greek Additions to Esther. The reader must understand and be aware of all the range of moral qualities in the literature in order to focus on specific contexts within the texts and thus move toward meaning.

The Greek word *praus*, then, belongs within the category of positive moral qualities: what is good, kind, just, holy, perfect, humble, gentle, blessed, merciful. To investigate use of the term within this semantic domain enables us to understand it in this wider environment both elsewhere in the New Testament and in the wider Greek-speaking world of the time. When the Hellenistic reader of Greek texts read the term *praus*, what was heard and understood was the sense of that term in a particular context for that reader. Accordingly, this book contains a synchronic study of *praus* in ancient Greek texts, particularly those of the New Testament and early Christian literature.[19]

Matthew and Moral Qualities

Matthew uses the word *praus* three times in the Gospel. Two of these occasions (5:5 and 21:5) are citations from the Hebrew Scriptures. One of the citations is from the Psalter (Ps. 36:11 in Matt. 5:5), and the other is a prophetic text (Zech. 9:9 in Matt. 21:5). Since these texts are appropriated from Hebrew Scriptures, the context in which to try and understand them is the one in which Matthew places them, namely, the Gospel. This means that I am not going to be looking for the meaning of Zechariah 9:9 for the Gospel within the wider context of Zechariah.[20] The meaning of the words of these texts would be understood as such terms were understood in Matthew's day. However, each use in the Gospel

---

18. Louw and Nida, *Greek-English Lexicon*, 1:761–63.

19. In 1915 Saussure proposed two sciences of language: diachronic or evolutionary linguistics and synchronic or static linguistics.

20. Unless I misunderstand him, John J. Collins, *The Scepter and the Star: The Messiahs of the Dead Sea Scrolls and Other Ancient Literature* (New York: Doubleday, 1995), 206–7, imports the full context of Zechariah 9:9 to supply meaning to Matthew 21:5 to read the description of Jesus not as "a different kind of Messiah" but as a militaristic Davidic messiah. If Matthew intended this reading, then why not cite Zechariah 9:9 and 10?

carries different connotations. Moreover, the immediate context of
a word does not supply the exclusive meaning. The same words
resonate with and inform each other within the Gospel.

A semantic domain, as we have seen, includes contrasting
as well as shared meanings. Matthew's usage of this domain is
pointed. Unlike the Additions to Esther, Matthew's Gospel juxtaposes moral qualities with their opposites: good/bad (or evil), just/
unjust, sin/righteousness, blessed/cursed, merciful/merciless. While
it is true that words are often understood by means of opposites,
Matthew's predilection for contrasting moral qualities belongs to a
world of apocalyptic eschatology. One age contrasts with another.
Matthew's Gospel characterizes the present age and its inhabitants
as evil in contrast to a coming age of righteousness. For Matthew's
Gospel, however, the resonance of this thought lies in the Gospel's depiction of conflict between the kingdom of heaven and the
kingdom of Satan.[21] Contrast informs the use of kingship language.

Matthew's Gospel opens with the identification of Jesus as one
belonging to the Davidic line. He is then recognized as "king of the
Jews" by Gentiles who do homage to him. The ruling king, Herod,
displays only hostility. The behavior of Joseph, a just man, who
does not wish to make an example of a woman (1:19), contrasts
with that of Herod, who makes an example of his intended homage
to the baby (2:8) the treatment of the defenseless male children
(2:16). The Gospel describes the character of Jesus' kingship in the
light of God's rule as one of humility and service. Other kings "lord
it over" their subjects. We will explore this further in chapter 4.

The description of personal qualities in Matthew's Gospel helps
to remind us that studying moral qualities in any text is not studying a list of abstractions. Sometimes modern handbooks discussing
values in the world of late antiquity or the time of the New Testament give this impression.[22] When we speak of qualities or values,
we usually assign them to a person (she is good) or the goal of an
action (that was the right thing to do). This is also true of Matthew's Gospel. People in it are good or bad, wise or foolish, and
there are just or unjust actions.

Matthew's Gospel belongs to a world in which there are slaves
and masters, kings and servants. The thoughts and actions of these
people can be evaluated in the light of moral qualities. While we

21. M. Eugene Boring, "The Gospel of Matthew," in *The New Interpreter's
Bible*, 12 vols. (Nashville: Abingdon, 1994–), 8:114–18.
22. John J. Pilch and Bruce J. Malina, eds., *Biblical Social Values and Their
Meanings: A Handbook* (Peabody, Mass.: Hendrickson, 1993).

might imagine that kings and slaves would be located in palaces, Matthew locates the action of good and bad kings or good and bad servants outside throne rooms. The setting Matthew most seems to favor when describing the actions of individuals, including servants and kings, is the household. Since humans create social institutions like that of the household in order to actualize values, this implies that for Matthew values are realized within such an institution. That is to say, values are realized not within the individual but within relationships. First-century society, unlike our modern western one, functions not as an aggregation of individuals but as a collection of interactive kinship groups.

The household in the ancient world is not the same as a house or an apartment or even a family today. The household in Matthew's time was a physical space populated by a lord or master of the household (a householder) and members of the household, including wives, children, and slaves together with what we would call members of the extended family and their slaves. There might be an overseer of servants to manage the household, particularly if it was large. In addition to the house itself, the householder owned property. This property might be a vineyard from which one could earn a living. The overseer managed the servants planting and harvesting the vineyard.[23]

Aristotle regards the household as the basic unit of the state or city consisting of four aspects: three relationships (husband-wife; father-children; master-slave) and the task of earning wealth.[24] The structure is hierarchical in that the householder rules over the others in the household, and it is patriarchal in that the husband controls and provides for the household. In Matthew's Gospel, Jesus is born in a house (2:11). The household into which Jesus is born contains the same elements but reconstitutes them. Joseph, for example, although he is never called "father" or "master," is the husband of Mary (1:16, 19). He never rules over the household, but he provides for them (by paying attention to divine intervention) both in Egypt (2:14) and in Nazareth (2:23). And the household into which Jesus is born has great wealth (2:11).

For Matthew, kings and servants, householders and slaves are

---

23. Matthew introduces household imagery into the discussion of Jesus with the Canaanite woman when the woman speaks of the dogs eating the crumbs from *the master's* table (15:27). This was first pointed out to me by Annie Russell in an exegesis of this passage.

24. Aristotle *Pol.* 1.2.1–2. Cited in Warren Carter, *Households and Discipleship: A Study of Matthew 19–20* (Sheffield: Sheffield Academic Press, 1994), 20.

18 *Jesus the Meek King*

potentially bad or good, just or unjust. This is a bit more complicated than saying (as we might easily do) that humans are a mixture of good and bad. To be sure, in Matthew's community good and bad exist side by side, so in a sense the community is a mixture of good and bad. But within the community individuals often behave in contradictory fashion; Matthew says on several occasions that people seem to be one thing but are another or that they say one thing but do another.[25] This kind of contradiction Matthew deplores. It is a duplicity within some humans no one should emulate. Such human moral duplicity evokes outrage and curses.

One can encourage kings and rulers to be beneficent and compassionate, knowing that of course despots and tyrants exist. Matthew does not present kings either as ideal rulers or as tyrants. Instead he subverts the office of leadership. Jesus teaches in Matthew's Gospel that those who wish to be first must be servants of all. This aspect of Matthew's presentation is in accord with the way Jesus' teaching is presented in the other Gospels. At the same time, and to a degree not found in other Gospels, Matthew emphasizes the office of king as a slave, and he places Jesus in both roles. The strategies by which Matthew casts Jesus as king include the genealogy (in which Jesus is placed within the messianic lineage of David); the identity of Jesus as "king of the Jews"; and the fulfillment of messianic passages from the Hebrew Scriptures (particularly Zechariah 9:9, cited in fulfillment of Jesus' entry into Jerusalem as a royal king). A further means by which the Hellenistic ideology of kings is subverted is to situate Jesus as king over a realm that has permeable boundaries and that is inaugurated but not complete. Auxiliary strategies depict Jesus as a leader to whom other leaders like the ruler (9:18) and the Roman centurion defer.[26]

A study of values in Matthew might seem an oblique way to look at a text. Matthew's Gospel is surely a text written to relate the story of Jesus. Yet for Matthew Jesus embodies certain ways of living that reflect the values of Matthew's culture. In Matthew's Gospel Jesus says of himself, "I am *praus* and humble of heart." The narrator of the Gospel understands Jesus to say in 21:5, "Behold, your king comes to you *praus* and riding on an ass." What does Jesus mean when he speaks of himself as *praus*? Why should

---

25. Herod in Matthew 2; 6:1; 7:9–11; 23:3.
26. Matthew 8:5–8. The centurion recognizes Jesus as "under authority." See chapter 4 for discussion of Jesus' status as client king. Matthew's Gospel uses the actual term "leader" or "ruler" (Greek *hēgemōn*) only in regard to Pilate (e.g., Matt. 27:2).

meekness be associated with kingship? To answer these questions is to probe the values of the surrounding culture.

Dispositional Qualities

Paul and other writers of letters in the New Testament are concerned with the behavior of converts. These writers exhort them to practice certain kinds of conduct addressing them directly. In Paul's letters there are no stories about the good or bad actions of people such as we have seen in Matthew. Rather we find lists of qualities exemplifying new life in the Spirit. Sometimes accompanying these lists is a rationale for certain kinds of behavior. Through exhortation, and occasionally admonition, Paul hopes to sustain, and in some cases create, the new community.

What is the basis for appeal? It is the authority Paul has as founder and leader of the new communities. He employs the model of father and brother in relation to them, although on one occasion he appeals to the Thessalonians as a nurse to her children.[27] By writing to new members as brothers and sisters or children, Paul identifies them as members of the family of God. Using language of great affection in his earliest letter, for example, Paul exhorts and instructs "brothers beloved by God."[28] Clearly the mode of expression consolidates affinity between Paul and the new believers as between members of a family.

We can be a bit more specific. Paul prefers to address believers as *adelphoi*, "brothers," rather than as children. About half of the New Testament references to *adelphoi* belong to the Pauline corpus, wherein believers are identified as family. Thus, for example, Paul speaks to the Corinthians:

> I appeal to you, *adelphoi*, by the name of our Lord Jesus Christ, that all of you agree and that there be no dissensions among you, but that you be united in the same mind and the same judgment.[29]

Similarly the authors of Hebrews and the Epistle to James use *adelphoi* to address members of the community who are the re-

---

27. Wayne A. Meeks, *The First Urban Christians: The Social World of the Apostle Paul* (New Haven, Conn.: Yale University Press, 1983), 84–96; Abraham Malherbe, *Paul and the Thessalonians* (Philadelphia: Fortress, 1987). See also Galatians 4:19.
28. 1 Thessalonians 1:4.
29. 1 Corinthians 1:10.

cipients of these works.[30] In the Gospels this term is used almost exclusively in the context of the biological family; however, on one occasion Jesus does call the members of the community *adelphoi*.[31] Outside the New Testament, members of the community of the Dead Sea Scrolls are identified as brothers.[32] This usage is probably drawn from biblical references to all Israel as brothers, a usage that we know continued in the Greek-speaking world.[33] Hebrews 7:5 makes this explicit by interpreting the term "people" as "brothers":

> And those descendants of Levi who receive the priestly office have a commandment in the law to take tithes from the people, that is, from their brethren, though these also are descended from Abraham.

When he calls his letter recipients "brothers," Paul is not just using family language. He is drawing on a specific and well-known form of address by community members.[34] But the word is more than a direct address in ancient texts; it signals a topic. Paul refers to it in 1 Thessalonians 4:9, where he uses a compound, *philadelphia*, a portmanteau word combining "love" and "brother": "Now concerning brotherly love." In 4 Maccabees 13 this term is used of fraternal affection among the seven brother martyrs. Plutarch's treatise *On Brotherly Love* is another example of this

---

30. Hebrews 2:11; 3:1, 12; 7:5; 10:19; 13:22; James 1:2, 16, 19; 2:1, 5, 14; 3:1, 10, 12; 4:11; 5:7, 9, 10, 12, 19.

31. Matthew 23:8: "But you are not to be called rabbi, for you have one teacher, and you are all *adelphoi*."

32. 4QDa 6,21–7,2: "[Those brought into the Covenant] shall love each man his brother as himself; they shall succour the poor, the needy, and the stranger. A man shall seek his brother's well-being and shall not sin against his near kin. . . . They shall rebuke each man his brother according to the commandment." Geza Vermes, ed. and trans., *The Complete Dead Sea Scrolls in English* (London and New York: Penguin, 1997), 132.

33. E.g., Leviticus 10:6: "your brethren, the whole house of Israel"; 1 Chronicles 28:2 (King David speaks): "Hear me, my brethren and my people"; 2 Maccabees 1:1: "The Jewish brethren in Jerusalem and those in the land of Judea, to their Jewish brethren in Egypt: Greeting, and good peace" (all quotations are from the RSV).

34. Some older translations use "brethren" to translate *adelphoi*. Modern translations may substitute "beloved" or "brothers and sisters." The NRSV even translates Matthew 23:8: "But you are not to be called rabbi, for you have one teacher, and you are all students." The translations "beloved" or "students" masks the fraternal associations of the word. The Louw-Nida lexicon moves in this direction with the rendering of *philadelphia* as "affection for one's fellow-believer in Christ." "Fellow" has a broader connotation in today's English than even a wider understanding of the term "brother."

topic in the Hellenistic world.[35] There are, however, significant differences between the New Testament and Plutarch. While Plutarch describes biological brotherhood, Paul's understanding of the same term is that it incorporates different social groups and geographical areas. Plutarch grounds its character in nature while Paul simply assumes nonsanguine affinity. He speaks of brotherly love as being "taught by God."[36] Plutarch assumes a hierarchy of relationships: the elder brother, for example, takes precedence over the younger. Paul does not preserve such distinctions. A more recent convert is not afforded a lower place in the hierarchy of the group. Indeed, mutuality promoted by the advocacy of dispositional qualities is a hallmark of Paul's letters rather than, for example, hierarchy based on precedence in the faith. Like Plutarch, however, both Paul and Matthew propose to solve sibling or personal differences privately within the community, rather than in public. All three propose tolerance to a greater or lesser degree: one should forgive a sinning brother to avoid public shame or legal expense.

Use of this topic signaled by the term "brother/brothers" or "brotherly love" would evoke associations and expectations on the part of readers of ancient texts. Among those would be descriptions of conduct maintaining and enhancing fraternal relationships. Forms of this conduct include the dispositional virtues of humility and meekness. Thus we find Paul appealing to new members of the community to practice meekness as an enhancement of community life.[37] The same understanding is implicit in Matthew and the Epistle to James. In Matthew, as we have seen, Jesus identifies the community as "brothers," and among the members must be the hearers of 5:5: "Blessed are the meek, for they shall inherit the earth." In James new believers are addressed as brothers and exhorted to "be quick to listen, slow to speak, slow to anger for your anger does not produce God's righteousness. Therefore, rid yourselves of . . . wickedness and welcome with meekness the implanted word that has the power to save your souls."[38] These examples

---

35. Reidar Aasgaard, "Brotherhood in Plutarch and Paul: Its Role and Character," in *Constructing Early Christian Families*, ed. Halvor Moxnes (New York and London: Routledge, 1997), 166–82.

36. 1 Thessalonians 4:9.

37. Galatians 5:22–23: "By contrast, the fruit of the Spirit is love, joy, peace, patience, kindness, generosity, faithfulness, *prautēs*, self-control. There is no law against such things"; Galatians 6:1: "Brothers, if anyone is detected in a transgression, you who have received the Spirit should restore such a one in a spirit of *prautēs*. Take care that you yourselves are not tempted."

38. James 1:19–21.

demonstrate that the language of fraternal affection could be used in groups or associations.

Were these exhortations indicative of general ideas on brother-hood in contemporary society? One scholar suggests that brother-hood might have been the social relation that was least regulated internally and was thus the one that allowed the greatest possibilities for individual differences and, at the same time, for mutual tolerance and forgiveness.[39] All these topics will be explored in the next chapter.

---

39. Aasgaard, "Brotherhood in Plutarch and Paul," 180.

Chapter 2

BROTHERLY LOVE

The topic of fraternal affection (*philadelphia*) signals to readers of Paul, Plutarch, and 4 Maccabees a discussion of other subtopics: kinship rather than isolation, harmony rather than discord, and resolution of quarrels rather than estrangement. To resolve differences, reason and self-control rather than anger and enmity play a large part. In this subtopic, Plutarch commends *praotēs*. While neither Paul nor the author of 4 Maccabees is writing specifically about brotherly love, each draws upon the topic to promote other ends. Paul uses it to maintain and enhance a cooperative spirit among members of early Christian communities. The author of 4 Maccabees uses it to promote a picture of seven martyred brothers united in their resistance to the evil tyrant Antiochus. For both authors, brotherhood and religion go hand in hand.

All three authors view the topic of *philadelphia* as the antidote to dysfunctional relations between brothers or family members or between the family and the outside world. Plutarch views it as a restoration of the harmony between siblings and family members that had existed in an earlier age. Paul understands brotherly love to exemplify forbearance between community members and hence as that which builds up common life. The author of 4 Maccabees sees the fraternity of seven brothers as a rational bulwark against those passions that lead to transgressions of the Law. It enables them to stand firm against the threat of disorder and emotional turmoil in the world outside.

Threading its way through these same discussions is the issue of gender identity. Men must be taught the meaning and practice of filial affection. Scholars have come to understand that in the Hellenistic period gender is socially constructed.[1] Control of oneself or

---

1. The literature on this topic is vast. See Michel Foucault, *The History of Sexuality*, 3 vols. (New York: Vintage, 1985, 1986); David M. Halperin, J. J. Winkler,

of others defines what it means to be masculine in the extant Greek
and Latin literature from antiquity. Self-control is the warrant for
control of others. The struggle to attain self-mastery stands on a
sliding scale from most masculine to least masculine. Location on
the scale depends on men's actions or conduct in any situation.
Masculinity in the ancient world is an achieved state regardless of
anatomical sex.[2] Even from birth, things are unstable. The embryo
is a mingling of male and female seed in which various propor-
tions are possible. The gender of a newborn is not an absolute but
a point on a sliding scale depending on the type of seed that pre-
dominates or the section of the womb in which it lies. Thus the
nurture of the child becomes a matter of great importance.

The physician Soranus (d. 135 C.E.) gives specific instructions
for the nurse to stretch and shape newborn limbs. Careful bathing
and massaging of the head and nose make both conform to the de-
sirable shape. She thus eradicates long heads and flat noses. Along
with the head and nose, the penis receives particular attention. If
the foreskin fails to cover the glans properly it would be stretched
gently every day. Likewise, the nurse massages the scrotum. All this
is done "for the sake of comely form."[3] The text does not discuss
or express interest in whose judgments about form it reflects.

The rationale is clear: the nurse shapes and molds the child's
body with the aim of instilling obedience and docility. The forming
of bodies and the forming of character go hand in hand. Until the
adolescent male is capable of independent rational action, ideally
making a choice for self-control through subduing the emotions,
he must be kept in line. The first-century account by Philo of the
adolescent Moses learning to discipline his emotions demonstrates
this well.

> When [Moses] was now passing beyond the term of boyhood,
> his good sense became more active. He did not, as some,
> allow the lusts of adolescence to go unbridled, though the
> abundant resources which palaces provide supply number-
> less incentives to foster their flame. But he kept a tight hold

---

and F. I. Zeitlin, eds., *Before Sexuality: The Construction of Erotic Experience in
the Ancient Greek World* (Princeton: Princeton University Press, 1990); Joan E.
Hartman and Ellen Messer-Davidow, eds., *(En)Gendering Knowledge: Feminists in
Academe* (Knoxville: University of Tennessee Press, 1991).

    2. Hippokrates *On Generation* 6.7.749; Galen *Nat. Fac.* 2.636–38.

    3. Soranus, *Gynecology,* trans. O. Temkin (Baltimore and London: Johns Hop-
kins University Press, 1956), 2.32 [101]-34 [103].

on them with the reins, as it were, of temperance and self-control, and forcibly pulled them back from their forward course. And each of the other passions, which rage so furiously if left to themselves, [he] disciplined (*epraunen*) and assuaged and reduced to mildness; and if they did but gently stir or flutter he provided for them heavier chastisement than any rebuke of words could give; and in general he watched the first directions and impulses of the soul as one would a restive horse, in fear lest they should run away with the reason which ought to rein them in, and thus cause universal chaos. For it is these impulses which cause both good and bad — good when they obey the guidance of reason, bad when they turn from their regular course into anarchy.[4]

This long paragraph demonstrates well the exercise of self-discipline in the creation and sustaining of masculinity in the Hellenistic period. Good qualities or virtues such as self-control rein in adolescent urges. Using the verb *praunō*, Philo depicts Moses disciplining and controlling the passions. Because the idea of taming is present in the verb, we see in the paragraph the image of a domestic animal in harness. Finally, note the value attached to the exercise of becoming a man. Disciplined impulses subject to reason result in good things while untrained passions cause bad.

The idea of training oneself to exercise the virtues goes back at least to Aristotle, and such Hellenistic authors like Isocrates and Plutarch refer to these older discussions.[5] There are both intellectual and moral virtues, according to the philosopher: wisdom, understanding, and prudence are intellectual virtues, whereas liberality and temperance are moral virtues. It is the moral virtues that describe a person's character. Philosophical texts like those of Aristotle and Plato praise virtues in general and in particular self-control, justice, and courage. Commending quiet virtues like *praotēs* implicitly challenges an older value system of competitive virtues found in the Homeric epics.

According to Aristotle, none of the moral virtues exist in us naturally. One may accrue intellectual virtues through instruction,

---

4. Philo *Moses* 1.25–27, trans. F. H. Colson, in *Philo* 4, Loeb Classical Library (Cambridge, Mass.: Harvard University Press, 1966), 289–91.

5. Plutarch, for example, specifically refers to Aristotle's discussion of the mean in his treatise *De virt. morali* (*Moralia* 440D–452D) 444E. On Plutarch generally, see Hans-Dieter Betz, ed., *Plutarch's Ethical Writings and Early Christian Literature*, Studia ad Corpus Hellenisticum Novi Testamentum 4 (Leiden: Brill, 1978).

"but their full development is due to habit."[6] The acquisition of
virtues is similar to what happens when someone learns to play
an instrument. Just as a good harpist becomes one through play-
ing the harp, so a temperate person becomes temperate[7] by doing
temperate things. Thus, since similar activities produce similar dis-
positions, the habits we form from the earliest age are extremely
important. Because moral goodness is a question of habituation,
true education is the training from infancy to feel joy and grief at
the right things. At this point, Aristotle articulates a principle of
right action: it must avoid both excess and deficiency even while it
is impossible to specify exactly what this would look like in every
situation.[8]

The discussion illustrates this principle through application of
specific virtues to particular cases on the grounds that "particular statements are closer to the truth."[9] In regard to self-control,
for example, the excess on one hand is licentiousness and on the
other something one might class as insensibility. Aristotle describes
the mean for each of the named virtues, placing on one side the
named excess and on the other the named deficiency. *Praotēs* is
the medium between anger and lack of spirit. In spite of these
examples, the discussion concludes by acknowledging that a person's temperament makes it difficult to specify the mean in every
situation. Aristotle proffers three general rules: avoid the extreme
more contrary to the mean; notice our natural tendencies and pull
hard in the opposite direction; guard against pleasure and pleasant
things since we are not impartial judges of pleasure.[10]

Study of another moral quality, self-control, suggests that, like
virtue or excellence in general, the same quality may apply to men
and women but that in regard to either it takes on different connotations. From its first uses in Homer, for example, the practice
of self-control is the activity of checking some natural impulse
through the exercise of will. The essential meaning is keeping one's
physical and psychological boundaries. Thus female self-control includes and sometimes is no more than chastity. Aristotle agrees that
women have self-control, but for them it is dutifulness and obedience. Since a woman cannot control herself, her self-control must

---

6. Aristotle *Eth. Nic.* 1103B.
7. This word has been translated elsewhere as "self-control."
8. Aristotle *Eth. Nic.* 1104A.
9. Ibid., 1107A.
10. Ibid., 1109A–B.

consist in submitting herself to the control of others.[11] For men it is rational self-control and resistance to excess.

We can see this exemplified in 4 Maccabees, where the brothers' exhibition of self-control in the face of torture and death is seen as manly.[12] In contrast, the male authority figure Antiochus exhibits the emotions of fury and anger. Going beyond Aristotle, 4 Maccabees depicts the self-mastery of the mother.

Plutarch seems to understand that affection between family or household members is both natural and also requires effort. Bonds between parents and children, husband and wife, friends and comrades represent a special kind of *praos* devotion.[13] In contrast to the Stoic search for an existence free of passion, Plutarch seeks to control and subdue emotions rather than transcend them:

> (Reason) does not wish to eradicate passion completely (for that would be neither possible nor expedient) but puts on it some limitation or order and implants the ethical virtues, which are not the absence of passion but a due proportion and measure therein; and reason implants them by using prudence to develop the capacity for passion into a good acquired disposition.[14]

The triumph of reason over passion and other feelings is not just the result of effort, for effort is expended in the enhancement of certain traits of character naturally present in the individual. A pleasant and happy life has its source in a man's character. His character adds the element of pleasure and joy to the things surrounding him. Wealth is more pleasant, "and so too men bear poverty, exile, and old age lightly and gently in proportion to the serenity and *praotēs* of their character."[15]

Kinship

In his essay *De fraterno amore (On Brotherly Love)*, Plutarch describes brothers as naturally united as the fingers on one hand. "It

---

11. Aristotle *Pol.* 1260A 20–24; 1277B 20–24.
12. Stephen D. Moore and Janice Capel Anderson, "Taking It Like a Man: Masculinity in 4 Maccabees," *Journal of Biblical Literature* 117/2 (1998): 249–73.
13. He expands this topic in essays on the tranquility of the soul and the control of anger, which we shall explore elsewhere.
14. Plutarch *De virt. morali* 443C–D.
15. Plutarch *De virt. et vitio* 100D.

is our very need," he says, "which welcomes and seeks friendship and comradeship, that teaches us to honor and cherish and keep our kin, since we are by nature unable and unfitted to live friendless, unsocial, and hermits' lives."[16] Nothing pleases parents more or prolongs their old age than the affection of their sons for each other. Most friendships reflect the first natural affection in children for their parents and for each other. Similarly in Paul, the promotion of cooperative qualities is an expression of brotherhood. Paul comports himself toward the new communities not as a tyrant but as a compassionate sibling. His use of affective language expands the emotional reservoir of the topic of brotherly love.

In 4 Maccabees, all of the seven brothers are tortured to death by the servants of Antiochus because they refuse to abandon the religion of their ancestors. Several make speeches before they are killed that illustrate their affiliation to ancestral religion and to each other. The eldest brother provides the first example of courage on the basis of fraternal bonds: "Imitate me, brothers," he said. "Do not leave your post in my struggle or renounce our courageous brotherhood."[17] The third, having been led in and asked to eat pork, shouts: "Do you not know that the same father begot me as well as those who died, and the same mother bore me, and that I was brought up on the same teachings? I do not renounce the noble kinship that binds me to my brothers."[18] The argument here is that similar origins nurture similar character. The fourth brother takes an oath: "No, by the blessed death of my brothers, by the eternal destruction of the tyrant, and by the everlasting life of the pious, I will not renounce our noble brotherhood."[19] The sixth brother makes the same argument: "I am younger in age than my brothers but I am their equal in mind. Since to this end we were born and bred, we ought likewise to die for the same principles."[20] After the horrible deaths of the brothers have been recorded, the narrator praises their resolve. They have shown that "devout reason is sovereign over the emotions."[21] To account for their fortitude,

---

16. Plutarch *De frat. amor.* 479C.
17. 4 Maccabees 9:23. Here the RSV is used. The NRSV translates "family ties" for "brotherhood" (Greek *adelphotēs*), thereby obscuring the connection to the topic of brotherly love.
18. 4 Maccabees 10:2–3.
19. 4 Maccabees 10:15. Again the translation is from the RSV for the same reason as in note 17.
20. 4 Maccabees 11:14–15.
21. 4 Maccabees 13:1.

the narrator refers directly to the topic of *adelphotēs* (brotherhood) and expounds its meaning for the resolve of the brothers:

> You are not ignorant of the affection of brotherhood which the divine and all-wise Providence has bequeathed through the fathers to their descendants and which was implanted in the mother's womb. There, each of the brothers spent the same length of time.... When they were born after an equal time of gestation, they drank milk from the same fountains. From such embraces, brotherly-loving souls are nourished; and they grow stronger from this common nurture and daily companionship, and from both general education and our discipline in the law of God.[22]

The narrator insists that the establishment of brotherly affection makes the brothers more sympathetic to one another. But in this case, the fraternal bonds are strengthened by education and religion. "Since they had been educated by the same law and trained in the same virtues and brought up in right living, they loved one another all the more."[23] In the end, however, while nature and customs augment brotherly affections, religion enables onlookers to endure the sufferings of the brothers. Moreover, the onlookers themselves enabled the brothers to despise their agonies and to control the emotions of *philadelphia*.[24]

Harmony

Another aspect of *philadelphia* emerges from this passage in 4 Maccabees 13, namely, harmony. In that passage there are a number of words signifying harmony. They include concord (*symphōnia*) and chorus (*choros*), together with their opposites: discord (*eris, machē*) and cacophony (*kakōphonia*). These words signal this subtopic. The unity of actions and resolve of the seven brothers causes the narrator of 4 Maccabees when explaining their *philadelphia* to exclaim: "O sacred and harmonious concord (*symphōnia*) of the seven brothers on behalf of religion!"[25] Obviously, the exclamation expresses admiration and relief that no one became an apostate. None of the seven brothers avoided torture and death. Even before the tortures begin, they speak with one

---

22. 4 Maccabees 13:19–22.
23. 4 Maccabees 13:24.
24. 4 Maccabees 14:1.
25. 4 Maccabees 14:3.

voice as from one mind: "Why do you delay, O tyrant? We are ready to die rather than distress our ancestral commandments."[26] The narrator goes on to liken their blessed harmony to seven days of creation "moving in choral dance around religion." The youths, forming a chorus, circle the sevenfold fear of torture and dissolve it.[27]

This leads into a discussion of the maternal sympathy of the mother of the seven sons. Through reason the mother conquers natural affection for her sons, and she witnesses the horrible death of each. Reason gives her heart a man's courage in the midst of her emotions. This strengthens her to disregard, for a time, her parental love.[28] Her resolve strengthens the unity of witness. She becomes the converse of the tyrant in the story: a woman controlling her emotions and maternal affections becomes male while the male ruler controlled by his emotional outbursts of anger against the brothers becomes female. The story ends on a note of harmony with the punishment of Antiochus. The sons of Abraham and the seven brothers with their victorious mother are gathered together into the chorus (*choros*) of the fathers, having received pure and immortal souls from God.[29]

According to Plutarch, nature gives brothers goodwill and *symphōnia*. They naturally desire to help one another. This harmony has a wide effect: "through the concord of brothers, family and household are sound and flourish, and friends and intimates, like a harmonious choir, neither do or say or think anything discordant."[30]

According to Plutarch, brotherly love is a proof of love for one's parents. Children learn brotherly love from the example of their father's love for his brother(s). It is absurd for a father who has fought with his brothers all his life to exhort his children to harmony. Brothers are irreplaceable, as may be seen from the example of a Persian woman choosing to save her brother in place of her children on the grounds that she could get other children but not another brother since both her parents were dead.[31]

---

26. 4 Maccabees 9:1.
27. 4 Maccabees 14:7–8; the quote is from verse 7.
28. 4 Maccabees 15:1, 22–23.
29. 4 Maccabees 18:23.
30. Plutarch *De frat. amor.* 479A. Elsewhere (Plutarch *De frat. amor.* 480–81) he gives a strange etymology of the name for the three Muses: from their being "always together" (*homou ousas*) in concord and *philadelphia*.
31. Ibid., 481E.

Resolving Quarrels

But all brothers do not exemplify *philadelphia*. In 4 Maccabees no
dissension between the seven brothers exists. They are united in
their opposition to the king. But they might not have been, and
the author imagines what arguments might have been used by the
brothers if some of them had been cowardly and unmanly. They
might decide to obey the king either through fear of torture or out
of compassion for their mother.[32] Had any one of the seven brothers failed to be steadfast, *philadelphia* would have been replaced
by discord and dissension.

The subtopic of dissension occupies most of Plutarch's treatise.
He seems most concerned about sibling arguments over inheritance. In proposing more appropriate conduct, Plutarch advocates
considerable self-control. Quarrels and arguments between children while the parents are alive deprive the warring siblings of the
greatest and fairest of legacies, the goodwill of parents. When, for
example, a father's anger is directed at one son, it is proper for any
other sons to treat the anger directed at their brother as directed
at them as well. Only after the erring brother has been defended
in this manner should the others turn to him and rebuke him with
confidence, pointing out his errors. A brother should not have free
rein, nor should he be trampled on when at fault. One should apply admonition "as one who cares for a brother and grieves for
him."[33] If a brother has done nothing wrong, even though it is right
to be subservient to parents and to endure their wrath and displea-
sure, pleas and justifications offered to the parents on behalf of the
brother are not wrong but honorable.

After the father's death, contention and strife between brothers
over the inheritance should be avoided. Instead one should rejoice
at surpassing a brother in fairness, generosity, and compliance.
To illustrate his point, Plutarch tells the story of Athenodorus.
When his elder brother Xenon squandered a substantial part of
Athenodorus's estate and brought public disgrace upon the family, Athenodorus did not neglect his brother after restitution of
the money but apportioned it between them. Even though he was
being treated unfairly in the division, "meekly (*praos*) and cheer-
fully he endured his brother's folly, which had become notorious
throughout Greece."[34]

---

32. 4 Maccabees 8:16–26.
33. Plutarch *De frat. amor.* 483A–B.
34. Plutarch *De frat. amor.* 484B. This is the use of the adverb.

For Plutarch, brotherly love has characteristic traits. It results from natural affinities and a common origin. Both elder and younger brothers should be deferential toward each other. To the elder brother Plutarch commends a spirit of philanthropy: the solicitude of a comrade rather than a father, and of one who persuades rather than commands. Since it is fitting for the young to respect their elders, Plutarch commends to the younger obedience and respectfulness. Imitation, not rivalry, is an appropriate attitude for the younger brother since it intimates admiration, not envy. Cato, for example, was so successful in winning over his elder brother Caepio "by obedience, *praotēs,* and silence" from their childhood onward that by the time both were adults Cato had filled his brother with so great a respect for himself that Caepio would not do or say anything without Cato's knowledge.[35]

"Nature," Plutarch says, "has given us *praotēs* and forbearance" to make the utmost of these virtues with our family and relatives.[36] The day of a quarrel should be forgotten. Goodwill and affection are promoted as much by our asking forgiveness for our own errors as our granting it to others when and even before they err. We should not overlook but try to forestall the anger of others. Once again, Plutarch gives an example. In the case of King Eumenes II of Pergamon, a deed revealed a *praotēs* no one could surpass. King Perseus of Macedonia had him ambushed, and although great stones fell on him, he lay not dead but stunned. News of his alleged death reached Pergamon. Attalus, the eldest of the king's brothers, not only took the crown but also married the king's wife. When news came that Eumenes was still alive, Attalus laid aside the crown and went to meet the king. Eumenes, for his part, not only grasped his brother's hand cordially but also embraced the queen with honor and friendliness. He went on living some time after his return without giving a hint of blame or suspicion. After his death, he left Attalus both his wife and his kingdom. For his part, Attalus set aside his own children and brought up and educated his brother's son. In his lifetime he placed the crown on his nephew's head and saluted him as king.

It is within the subtopic of dissension between brothers that Paul's use of the term *philadelphia* occurs. Both Paul and Plutarch use the same language.[37] In Romans 12:10, for example, Paul

35. Ibid., 487C.
36. Ibid., 489C.
37. It is not that Paul or Plutarch borrows from the other but that they use the

enjoins readers to "love one another with *philadelphia.*"[38] This exhortation follows the advice that everyone "among you not think more highly than you ought." In Romans 14–15, there is an extended discussion of weaker and stronger brothers, based on food regulations. "Some believe in eating anything, while the weak eat only vegetables."[39] Like Plutarch, Paul believes the stronger brother should defer to the conscience of the weaker and not injure him by what is eaten. He uses the language of harmony to promote this end: "Let us pursue what makes for peace and for mutual upbuilding."[40]

Paul uses *prautēs* twice in letters to the Corinthian community. An important purpose of his letters to the Corinthians is reestablishing his personal authority in that community, which he had established around 51 C.E. From 1 Corinthians itself we know he was not acting alone but in concert with others: Prisca, Aquila, and Apollos. From this letter it is possible to deduce some beliefs at Corinth about which Paul expresses concern: the Corinthians seem to believe themselves in full possession of the benefits of the resurrection. Individuals at Corinth demonstrate an abundance of spiritual gifts. These people show contempt for those in whom they are not evident. They do not respect Paul's leadership.

To invoke his authority as founder of the community, Paul uses paternal and maternal metaphors:[41] he has been wet nurse to the Corinthians (1 Cor. 3:2) and their only father (4:14–21):

> I am not writing this to make you ashamed, but to admonish (*noutheteō*) you as my beloved children. For though you might have ten thousand guardians in Christ, you do not have many fathers. Indeed, in Christ Jesus through the gospel I begot you. I appeal to you, then, be imitators of me. For this reason I sent you Timothy, who is my beloved and faithful child in the Lord, to remind you of my ways in Christ Jesus, as I teach them everywhere in every church. But some of you, thinking that I am not coming to you, have become arrogant.

same vocabulary since they ground their appeal in the benefits of brotherly love. Like Plutarch, Paul must have had an education in rhetoric. C. Forbes, "Comparison, Self-Praise, and Irony in Paul's Boasting and the Conventions of Hellenistic Rhetoric," *New Testament Studies* 32 (1986): 1–30.

38. Again the RSV translation is followed. The NRSV translates *philadelphia* as "mutual affection."

39. Romans 14:2.

40. Romans 14:19.

41. These metaphors appear elsewhere in Paul's letters but without the use of *praotēs*. In Galatians 4:19 he uses the maternal imagery of the pains of childbirth.

But I will come to you soon, if the Lord wills, and I will find out not the talk of these arrogant people but their power. For the kingdom of God depends not on talk but on power. What would you prefer? Am I to come to you with a stick, or with love in a spirit of *prautēs?*

Paul's appeal to the Corinthians is on the basis of his relationship to them as a parent. As such, he employs persuasion based on compassion and affection rather than coercion, the method of a teacher or a guardian. But he implies that he *could* use force. At the same time, he sets himself up as rival to those among the Corinthians he calls arrogant. As rival, he is in a sense their sibling. Thus, although the basis of his appeal evokes the familial bonds of parent and child, his appeal to them uses the language of fraternal affection as that of an elder to a younger brother.

We have already seen Plutarch's description of the ideal behavior of an elder brother to the younger: to be solicitous, to lead and admonish, and to persuade rather than command.[42] Both Plutarch and Paul use the Greek verb *noutheteō*. Elsewhere Plutarch advises brothers to be as well-disposed to their nephews as to their own children and perhaps even more gentle[43] and tender, so that when they err as they undoubtedly will, they may not run away or associate with undesirable folk but have recourse and refuge that admonishes in a kindly way and intercedes for their offenses.[44] To admonish in a context of familial affection is never done harshly but always with the intent to restore the individual to the family group.

Plutarch, as we have seen, advises the younger brother to imitate rather than rival the elder.[45] Similarly Paul, using the same Greek verb, urges the Corinthians to imitate him. Plutarch's explanation of the desired effect from the appeal to fraternal affection illustrates what Paul hopes to achieve from his audience: obedience, together with respect bringing about goodwill and favor, which will in turn lead to concessions.

Paul's appeal to the Corinthians on the basis of his relationship to them as father or elder brother appears again at 2 Corinthians 10:1:

---

42. Plutarch *De frat. amor.* 487B.
43. This is the Greek word *ēpios,* one of the words under the subdomain of moral qualities in the Louw-Nida lexicon. For discussion, see chapter 1.
44. Plutarch *De frat. amor.* 491E–F.
45. Ibid., 487B.

I myself, Paul, appeal to you by the *prautēs* and gentleness (*epieikeia*) of Christ — I who am humble when face to face with you, but bold toward you when I am away!

Paul's presence at Corinth has been seen by some as humble in a malicious sense, that is, insignificant or weak. At 10:10 he quotes this opinion: "For they say: 'His letters are weighty and strong but his bodily presence is weak and his speech contemptible.' " Hence Paul's mention of the *prautēs* and gentleness of Christ is the basis for his own appeal. This can only be made by arguing that the *prautēs* and gentleness of Christ is power. In 1 Corinthians 1:18 and elsewhere Paul defends the notion that the message about the cross seems foolish, but to those who are being saved, it is the power of God.

This argument is made with a specifically theological emphasis by the author of the second-century *Epistle to Diognetus* 7.3–4[46] to describe the sending of Christ by God:

Now was [Christ] sent, as anyone might suppose, in tyranny, fear and terror? Not so, but in gentleness and *prautēs* [God] sent him, as a king sending his royal son. He sent him as sending God; as a human to humans; He was saving and per-suading [when he sent him], not compelling, for compulsion is not an attribute of God.

The use of familial language in this passage is in the image of father and son. While a king might be expected to be despotic and the son to be princely, the son is sent instead "as a human to humans," to persuade and not coerce. How does he fail to compel? By not appearing as king. So Paul does not appear to be bold or strong to some at Corinth. All the same, just as the king's son does not appear as a king but is one, so Paul does not seem to be strong but is so. Yet instead of being bold in his presence at Corinth, Paul makes a virtue of his weakness. He is able to achieve far more by persuasion than he would through coercion. Thus the weakness of Paul and that of other apostles is the direct continuation of the foolishness of the cross and the willing humiliation of Jesus. For Paul, the *prautēs* and gentleness of Christ is an attitude shown in the state of humility and weakness. Jesus demonstrates *prautēs* and gentleness by becoming humble and weak.[47]

46. H. G. Meecham, *The Epistle to Diognetus* (Manchester: Manchester University Press, 1949), 495.

47. Ragnar Leivestad, " 'The Meekness and Gentleness of Christ': II Cor X,1," *New Testament Studies* 12–13 (1966) 156–64.

Conclusion

In the Hellenistic world, the topic of brotherly love includes the themes of kinship, harmony, and lack of dissent. In 4 Maccabees and in Plutarch's treatise *De fraterno amore*, these virtues function to identify and strengthen fraternal ties between those who are persecuted and those who contribute to the stability of society. In such situations, males attain degrees of self-control. While adolescent males must learn how to become male through the disciplining of the emotions, self-control and reason teach men how to comport themselves in the face of unstable situations like imprisonment and threat of torture.

In Paul's letters to the Corinthians and his advice to the stronger brother(s) in Romans 14–15, we see a development of the subtopic of dissension between brothers. To a divided community, Paul advocates harmony. Between brothers, Paul instructs the stronger to defer to the conscience of the weak.

A different use of the same motif appears in Paul's letters. He knows not the life but the death of Jesus. His is not the historical Jesus but the risen Christ. Paul cannot, as Philo can in regard to Moses, point to any occasion in which Jesus acts out character traits or virtues in his life. For him, the meekness of Jesus is a state realized not in the quality of his life but in his manner of death. Paul takes the ignominious manner of Jesus' death and uses it to address charges that his own physical presence is weak. Jesus' humility in death is a counterpart of his own humility and weakness in life. To oppose those he deems arrogant, he makes a virtue out of the weakness of his physical presence at Corinth. He articulates this appeal using the language of brotherly affection. His argument is made in the belief that the end is imminent and the time is short. As in the case of the brothers of 4 Maccabees, the figure of Christ for Paul exemplifies in death a virtue that sustains community.

In their treatment of *philadelphia*, there are many similarities between Plutarch and Paul. Both treat the idea of brotherhood as a discrete topic with practical implications for conduct. Both treat it as a topic with connection to family or household relations. To be sure, Plutarch's ideas are about flesh-and-blood brothers while Paul's are about members of communities. Moreover, Plutarch, like the author of 4 Maccabees, accounts for *philadelphia* by arguing for natural affection and common upbringing. Paul, who is not addressing a community of persons related biologically, cannot make the same argument and thus ignores the question of the origin of *philadelphia*. He assumes that it is part of the instruction of members of the communities but does not explain further. With regard to dissension, both Plutarch and Paul propose to resolve quarrels within the community. This avoids public humiliation resulting from possible resolution through litigation. Both Plutarch and Paul recognize the need to create harmony through the deference of brothers one to another. Paul, however, stresses the deference of the stronger to the younger brother for the sake of building up the community. For Plutarch, *praotēs* is the antidote to strife between brothers. This is similar to the argument of 2 Timothy 2:24–25: "And the Lord's servant must not be quarrelsome but kindly to everyone, an apt teacher, forbearing, correcting opponents with *prautēs*." Paul does not use *prautēs* in quite the same way. For Paul, there are many ways to resolve sibling conflict, including forbearance and admonishment. Rather, the *prautēs* of Christ is a justification for the (valid) accusation that Paul's presence at Corinth is weak.[48]

A woman may exhibit control of the emotions, especially affection. In one such case, the mother of the seven sons martyred for their religion under Antiochus is more manly than the ruling male. According to Plutarch, it is not natural for either men or women to be competitive or to be alone. While some texts, without disagreeing in principle, view women as somewhat contentious, others texts set them as models of quiet virtues for the community:

> Let [our wives] exhibit the lovely habit of purity, let them show forth the innocent will of *prautēs*, let them make the gentleness of their tongues manifest by their silence, let them not give their affection by factious preference, but in holiness to all equally who fear God.[49]

In such cases, the community already esteems virtues enhancing a cooperative spirit. So too in 1 Peter, women bring in their husbands to the new faith by means of their quiet conduct. Women are to accept authority not because it is intrinsically correct that

---

48. The author of 4 Maccabees does not use *prautēs*, since dissension in the text occurs between the heroes and the tyrant and not within the community. Moreover, deference would not suit an argument promoting rational determination in opposition to powerful tyranny.

49. 1 Clement 21.7; ET Kirsopp Lake, *The Apostolic Fathers*, 2 vols., Loeb Classical Library (Cambridge: Harvard University Press, 1959) 1:47.

their husbands should exert it but because the purity and reverence of their conduct may "win [their husbands] over without a word." That this is a long-standing practice is understood through the reference to the obedience of other holy women, including Sarah.[50]

---

50. 1 Peter 3:1; verse 6 refers to Sarah.

Chapter 3

HELLENISTIC KINGSHIP

The philosopher Isocrates intended his *Panegyricus* (380 B.C.E.) to call for a program of political action that would unite the Greek cities as a confederation. In 346 B.C.E. Isocrates spoke directly to Philip of Macedon, advocating that Philip liberate the Greek cities of the Anatolian coast under Persian control. It fell to Philip's son, Alexander, to realize that plan. In the eleven years between his crossing of the Hellespont in the spring of 334 and his death in Babylon on June 10, 323, Alexander changed the face of the ancient world forever. His military victories spread the political and social horizons of Greek society over vast tracts of land and sea, encompassing and blending with diverse peoples and tongues. Consolidation of Greek presence was achieved by the creation and maintenance of Hellenistic cities throughout these lands. These outposts were colonies of his power. New centers of learning came into being at Alexandria, Pergamon, and Antioch. Intellectual life at Athens received a new impetus.

The legacy of Hellenism itself is enormous. Among its monuments are the university, the catechetical school, pastoral poetry, monasticism, gnosticism, the romance, grammar, lexicography, city planning, theology, canon law, heresy, and scholasticism.[1] Perhaps the most important institution in the Hellenistic period is kingship.[2] In this chapter I will explore the notion of Hellenistic kingship and its legacy. This is a preface to a study of the topic in Matthew's Gospel. It is my contention that the demeanor and status of the Hellenistic king Herod the Great (a Roman client king)

---

1. F. E. Peters, *The Harvest of Hellenism: A History of the Near East from Alexander the Great to the Triumph of Christianity* (New York: Touchstone, Simon and Schuster, 1970), 23.

2. Per Bilde, Troels Engberg-Pedersen, Lise Hannestad, and Jan Zahle, eds., *Aspects of Hellenistic Kingship*, Studies in Hellenistic Civilization 7 (Oakville, Conn.: Aarhus University Press; Cambridge: Cambridge University Press, 1996), 9.

is set up as a foil to the demeanor and status of Jesus in Matthew's Gospel. Similarities exist in the attitudes of others toward them (see chap. 4). First, however, a description of Hellenistic kingship.

Since Alexander died without an effective successor, within twenty years of his death the empire had split into separate states whose ruler had taken the title of king.[3] No Greek (or person within the orbit of Alexander's empire) could henceforth avoid the influence of the monarchy. Whether written for the Attalids in Pergamon, the Ptolemies in Egypt, the Antigonids in Macedonia, or the Seleucids in Syria, political theory took account of this new reality. Kingship was the best form of state. In fact, the only Hellenistic state was a monarchy.[4]

The idea of monarchy was not novel. In places like Sparta there were kingdoms in modified forms, and the city-states of Asia Minor had been introduced to Persian kingship, but most city-states had not been subjected to the rule of monarchies for centuries. A philosophical discussion of monarchy, however, existed in Greece. According to Aristotle, kingship is the resource of the better classes against the people, whereas a tyrant is chosen from the people to be their protector against the nobles.[5] The institution of monarchy is best suited to defending the interests of the rich. For Plato, the best constitution was that giving power to the philosopher-kings,[6] but in *Politics* (294A) he proposed instead that a wisely conducted monarchy was superior to a constitution based on the rule of law. In the *Laws* (4.711E–712A) he argued that if a man with a "divine passion for self-control and justice" could be found, then the best thing to do was to hand the city over to him.

Such writings provided justification for the existence of Hellenistic kings. Macedonia and Achaemenia (Persia) had long existed under kings, and some Greek city-states, such as Sparta, had had restrained kingships. The idea of absolute monarchy, however, had not influenced the Greeks until Alexander's defeat of the king of the Achaemenians. After that victory, Alexander thought of himself not merely as the king's conqueror but as his successor as well. However, he did refuse to style himself Great King of Persia. Although

---

3. F. W. Walbank, "Monarchies and Monarchic Ideas," in *The Cambridge Ancient History,* vol. 7, 1 (Cambridge: Cambridge University Press, 1982), 62–100.

4. Victor Ehrenberg, *The Greek State,* 2d ed. (Oxford: Basil Blackwell, 1969), 159.

5. Aristotle *Pol.* VII (V). 10.3.1310B 9–12. Cited in Walbank, "Monarchies," 62.

6. Plato *Republic* 499B–C.

he donned the great king's purple tunic with its central white stripe and golden belt,[7] he shunned the full Achaemenid regalia because he wanted neither to be typecast as the archetypal oriental despot nor to be considered only as ruler of the former Persian empire. He was king of Asia. As we shall see, even these limited sartorial concessions to the conquered aroused considerable resentment in the army. This difficult situation lays bare the irresolvable contradiction at the heart of Alexander's imperial venture.

Alexander's successors, the Diadochoi, derived their understanding of the monarchy to a large degree from their Macedonian legacy. Monarchy was also based on personal achievement. As Alexander had conquered Asia by the spear, so also had these kings won their lands. Sons might succeed fathers and establish a dynasty, but it was still thought necessary to prove oneself on the battlefield.

The Hellenistic kings were not tied to any particular location, nor were they tied to the people. They did adopt local titles, but these titles meant nothing to the Greco-Macedonian people. However, they are of interest to this study. The Seleucid king Antiochus I is described in one source as "the powerful king, the king of the world, the king of Babylon, king of the lands,"[8] and the Ptolemies, as pharaohs, were kings of "Upper and Lower Egypt."[9] Only in Macedonia did the king sometimes go by the title "king of the Macedonians," but F. W. Walbank suggests that this title was used infrequently and probably only when the king wanted to make a special point.[10] Later Hellenistic rulers put the title before their names. One should not think of Macedonian rulers as differing drastically from their Hellenistic counterparts except that more treatises *On Kingship* seem to have been written for the early Antigonids than for the Ptolemies.

Part of the necessary glamor of kingship was secured by the wearing of special clothing and symbols of royalty, although compared with eastern monarchies this remained on a fairly modest level. Once Darius was dead, Alexander adopted some items of Per-

---

7. Ephippos in Athenaios, *Table Talk (Athenai Deipnosophistarum)*, ed. G. Kaibel (Leipzig: Teubner, 1908), 12.537e (Fragments of Greek Historians 126 F5); Plutarch *De Alexandri magni fortuna aut virtute* 2.2 (*Moralia* 329F–330A). Plutarch approves of this practice since it mollifies and tames (*praunō*) aggressive nations.

8. Walbank, "Monarchies," 66.

9. Ibid., 66; Walbank says (n. 12) that the Egyptian version is in E. A. Wallis Budge, *The Rosetta Stone in the British Museum* (London: AMS Press, 1929), pl. 3.

10. Walbank, "Monarchies," 65.

sian court dress. However, although he wore the diadem, he never wore the king's upright tiara. The Hellenistic kings wore Macedonian dress, which consisted of boots, a cloak, a broad-brimmed hat (or a helmet in war time), and purple robes. They also wore a diadem on the head or over the helmet, consisting of a purple-and-white or plain white headband with two loose ends. Occasionally they wore crowns, presented as an expression of gratitude by Greek cities, purple robes, a scepter, and a ring with a seal stone. Idealized representations of the king appeared in statues or on coins. It is to the idea behind the office that we now turn.

Sources for the Concept of the Ideal King

As indicated, philosophical resources for reflection on kingship were known from the fourth century. Isocrates wrote a laudatory biography of Evagoras, the king of Cyprus, and this was a model for Xenophon's encomium on the Spartan king Agesilaus. Among the latter's qualities are his virtues: he was god-fearing, just, generous, incorruptible, self-controlled in food and drink and sexual pleasures, courageous, patriotic, and the enemy of barbarians. Xenophon's work *Cyropaedia*, a fictional biography of Cyrus the Great, was a survey of qualities inherent in a good king. More influential than Xenophon were the writings of Isocrates: the address *Ad Nicoclem (To Nicocles)*, published shortly before Nicocles' accession of Cyprus in 374/3 and before the publication of the biography of his father Evagoras, and *The Nicocles*, an exhortation to his citizens placed in the mouth of Nicocles, urging the superiority of kingship over aristocracy and democracy because of its permanence and stability. A monarchy "is more agreeable and *praos* and just" than other models of government. Isocrates gives the example of Nicocles' replenishing of the royal treasury. At the same time, Nicocles says, "toward the citizens of the state I behaved with such *praotēs* that no one has suffered exile or death or confiscation of property or any such misfortune during my reign."[11] A benevolent monarch models behavior for his subjects.

A good illustration of the juxtaposition of competitive values with quieter ones in the Hellenistic period may be seen in Isocrates' encomium of Evagoras, a rhetorical eulogy written sometime after 374 B.C.E. Of course, the literary convention of a eulogy is to praise the achievements of the dead person. But at the conclusion,

---

11. Isocrates *Nicocles* or *The Cyprians* 32.

in a demonstration of the general excellence of Evagoras and in particular his courage and his wisdom, Isocrates praises the martial achievements through which he became king: the restoration of honor to his family, the transformation of the barbarians (i.e., non-Greeks into Greeks), and the civilizing and taming of a wild and inhospitable country.[12] That Isocrates praises Evagoras for the taming and domestication of a country alongside more traditionally competitive achievements such as war shows that both sets of values within the life of one educated ruler are thought commendable in the Hellenistic period. Isocrates says that he cannot choose which of these accomplishments is the greatest. He values military achievements and the subsequent rule by which Evagoras extends the benefits of Greek culture and society to non-Greeks.

How widely beyond philosophical circles the speculations of philosophers like Aristotle, Plato, and Isocrates were known is not clear. Monarchy was not an institution suited to the average Greek. It was a foreign institution with bizarre customs:

> Those [Persians], on the other hand, who stand highest in repute among them have never governed their lives by dictates of equality or of common interest or of loyalty to the state; on the contrary, their whole existence consists of insolence toward some, and servility toward others — a manner of life than which nothing could be more demoralizing to human nature. Because they are rich, they pamper their bodies; but because they are subject to one man's power, they keep their souls in a state of abject and cringing fear, parading themselves at the door of the royal palace, prostrating themselves, and in every way schooling themselves to humility of spirit, falling on their knees before a mortal man, addressing him as a divinity, and thinking more lightly of the gods than of men.[13]

Nevertheless, the appearance of the Hellenistic monarchies justified the creation of ideologies from the pens of Isocrates and others.

In fact, there once was a vast body of Hellenistic literature on kingship. One of the earliest was Aristotle's work *On Kingship*, perhaps written for Alexander on his accession to the throne. Although this work is no longer extant, we can glean ideas on kingship from other writings. From *Politics* we learn that though true

---

12. Isocrates *Evagoras* 65–67. The comparative of meek is used: "[Evagoras] made [the country] more civilized and *praoteron.*"
13. Isocrates *Paneg.* 151.

knowledge is possible only about universals, its equivalent in the sensory world, *phronēsis* (practical wisdom), "is the only virtue special to the ruler."[14] Aristotle notes that the absolute ruler would be "so surpassing in virtue and political power (*dunamis*) as to be like a god among men."[15] It is possible that this last remark describes Alexander.

Among the Stoics the subject of kingship was very popular, although all that remains are the titles attributed to Zeno, Cleanthes, Sphaerus, and Perseus, who wrote for the Antigonid kings. A few fragments of Theophrastus's treatise have survived.[16]

Happily, other works have survived from which it is possible to recover a general idea of kingship in the Hellenistic period. One source, written at the court of Ptolemy I probably before the end of the fourth century, derives from the historian and skeptic philosopher Hecataeus of Abdera's *On the Egyptians* and is found in the first book of Diodorus's *History*. The last section, describing the customs of the Egyptians, contains an idealized picture of Ptolemy, whose everyday routine is prescribed in minute detail according to sacred law and custom. The king is obliged to act so as to confer benefits on his people and thus win their gratitude. Hecataeus's picture is Greek. Egyptian ideas have been translated into Greek concepts.

The next source is the *Epistle of Aristeas*, purporting to explain the history of the Greek translation of the Hebrew Scriptures. At the request of Ptolemy II (285–246 B.C.E.) seventy-two elders of Israel, six from each tribe, translated the Hebrew Bible into Greek in seventy-two days in Alexandria. From this number the abbreviation (from the Roman numeral) LXX for the Septuagint derives. The account of the translation itself is brief. A large part of the text is given over to a description of a banquet given by Ptolemy at the completion of the work. In the course of the meal, the elders are asked questions concerning the nature and problems of kingship. Nuances of the answers do not prevent the account from being very informative about Hellenistic ideas of kingship. Walbank thinks it the best surviving source on the topic.[17]

There are also three pseudo-Pythagorean treatises on kingship preserved in Stobaeus. Comprising different sources, one stresses the resemblance of the king in his kingdom to God in the universe.

---

14. Aristotle *Pol.* 3.4.1277B 25–30.
15. Ibid., 3.7.1284A 10–12.
16. *P. Oxy.* 1611.
17. Walbank, "Monarchies," 78.

He is supreme commander, a dispenser of justice, and overseer of divine cults. These treatises may be used with caution. We can add to literary sources what can be gleaned from inscriptions and monuments of the period.[18] Antiochus I was the hereditary local ruler of Kommagene, a small but rich kingdom in eastern Anatolia. Like others of the Hellenistic world, he was a Hellenized Iranian with some Seleucid blood since his father had married a Seleucid princess. Upon the dissolution of Seleucid power in this region by the Romans in 64 B.C.E., Antiochus was left as Roman client king forming a buffer between Asia Minor and the Parthians. Antiochus seems to have conceived of his kingship as combining the best of Hellenic and Persian traditions. He instituted worship of himself and an assembly of mixed Greco-Asian gods at sanctuaries throughout his kingdom. The sanctuaries were furnished with large sculptured monuments and verbose cult inscriptions that tell in exalted style of his theocratic program. One reads thus:

> The Great King Antiochus, God Just and Manifest, Friend of the Romans, Friend of the Greeks . . . inscribed on consecrated bases with inviolable letters the deeds of his personal grace, for eternal time.[19]

Reflecting joint descent from Macedonian and Achaemenid royalty, the sculptural style seems likewise mixed. How typical of Hellenistic rulers Antiochus's inscriptions were is unclear.

At Alexandria, an enormous amount of marble sculpture has been recovered. Three heads from the Serapeion (the temple of Serapis) represent Serapis, a king, and a queen. They are probably from a royal cult group that featured a seated Serapis flanked by a standing king and queen. All three heads display a smooth, elevated, generalized appearance over iconographic specificity. The head of the king from this group shows an ideal royal style implicitly suggesting godlike qualities while remaining separate from more clearly divine images. The queen is likewise ideal but clearly not a goddess. Both have an elevated air designed to express the concern of rulers for their subjects, the royal virtue of *philanthrōpia* (philanthropy or generosity).[20]

---

18. Andrew Stewart, *Faces of Power: Alexander's Image and Hellenistic Politics* (Berkeley and Los Angeles: University of California Press, 1993).

19. R. R. R. Smith, *Hellenistic Sculpture* (London: Thames and Hudson, 1991), 227.

20. Ibid., 207 (fig. 227).

Regional Rulers

In Egypt, the monarchy acquired particular status. Around 280
B.C.E., after the death of his father, the new ruler Ptolemy II made
public — and international — declaration of the divinization of his
dead mother and father as "savior gods" (*theoi sōtērēs*). The practice was widely imitated throughout the Hellenistic monarchies,
except the Macedonian, and later among the Romans, where the
act of canonization was simultaneously a gesture of filial piety
and a cementing of the dynasty's claim to rule.[21] The suggestion of a dynasty was made. Ptolemy II and his wife Arsinoe
were called brother and sister. Other common cult names among
Hellenistic monarchs were Savior (*Sōtēr*), Benefactor (*Euergetēs*),
and God-made-manifest (*Epiphanēs*). Alexander himself was king
(*basileus*) of Macedon, later of all Asia, and leader (*hēgemōn*) of
the Greeks.[22]

In Macedon, where the divinization of rulers was and remained
an alien custom, the rule of the king was solidly grounded in the
popular will as expressed by the Macedonian army. Following Alexander's death, a short period of chaos presaged the ascent of
Gonatas to the Macedonian throne, where his family ruled un-
interruptedly for more than a century. After the defeat of the
Macedonian army at Pydna in 168 B.C.E., the Romans deported
Perseus, the last king of the Antigonid house, to Rome. In 148
B.C.E., the former kingdom was made into a Roman province.

Antigonus Gonatas, who had been an early student of Cynicism,
tried unsuccessfully to invite Zeno, the founder of Stoicism, to the
Macedonian court at Pella. Zeno, however, remained Gonatas's
friend for life and sent in his place his student Perseus, who was
appointed to serve as tutor of Gonatas's son and as the theoreti-
cian of Antigonid kinship. F. E. Peters surmises that what probably
emerged was a Stoic "Mirror for Princes" tempered by the realities
of the Macedonian political tradition.[23] Gonatas and his successors
disclaimed any association with the charismatic kingship of Alexander. So too did they shun the temptations of pharaonism that
worked so well in Egypt and even among the Seleucids.

For the Antigonids kingship was a natural bequest given by
the people to deserving individuals. In Perseus's phrase it was a
"noble servitude" performed for the good of the people by the

21. Peters, *Harvest of Hellenism*, 156.
22. Plutarch *Alexander* 27.6; 34.1.
23. Peters, *Harvest of Hellenism*, 91.

ruler. The army had the right to elect the king. The king, of course, ruled under the guidance of the Stoic sage. The Antigonids ruled at home modestly and simply in an age of divine kings and gods made manifest and faithfully followed the path charted by the undeified and restrained Gonatas down to the end with Philip V and his son Perseus. At first the monarchy turned on the dynastic claims of Philip II's family, but with the evaporation of that hope in the deaths of Philip III and Alexander IV the circle broadened to include Alexander's staff. These men were not only victorious generals but also members of a national elite, and from them Antigonus Gonatas emerged.

Royal Qualities

The military legacy of Alexander created expectations of martial excellence. Because the king or queen is victorious, he or she can protect his people and be their savior (*sōtēr*) and benefactor (*euergetēs*). The letter of Aristeas has one of the Jewish elders define the king's duty as "preserving the lives of people." In this sense, the monarch defends the nation against the tide of barbarism, as we have seen in the case of Isocrates' encomium of Evagoras. In times of war, a *praos* king is compassionate to the enemy, preferring to save rather than end their lives. Thus *praotēs* is an alternative to anger and retribution. But the greatest benefits a monarch can confer upon subjects is peace and justice. The last question put by Ptolemy II to the elders in the letter of Aristeas (291–92) was "What is the greatest thing in royalty?" The reply: "It is that the subjects may always enjoy peace and obtain justice promptly in the courts." Justice is a classic virtue. It is justice that Theophrastus has in mind when he says in his work *On Kingship* that the true king rules with the aid of the scepter rather than the sword.[24] Justice depends on the kings' obedience to the laws, "so that by practicing justice they may improve the lives of their peoples."[25]

Justice and wise administration demanded different qualities from those needed to defend the land from enemies. To maintain peace one must be *philanthrōpos* (generous) and *megalopsuchos* (magnanimous) in dealings with the people. Generosity or humanity was not a quality expected of rulers in the Homeric period or in classical writings, but *philanthrōpia* is one of the commonest

24. *P. Oxy.* 1611, lines 42–46.
25. *Ep. Arist.* 279.

words in the vocabulary of Hellenistic inscriptions, applicable to subjects and monarch alike.[26] The letter of Aristeas accounts the *philanthrōpia* and *agapēsis* (affection) of subjects as the supreme acquisition a king can possess.[27] Likewise, magnanimity (*megalopsuchia*) is an essential royal, quality. "The mistakes of private persons [Agesilaus] judged leniently, because few interests suffer by their incompetence; but the errors of rulers he treated as serious, since they lead to many troubles. Kingship, he held, demands not indolence, but manly virtue."[28] There are other virtues that a ruler must display. He or she must be pious toward the gods and affectionate and compassionate toward subjects. He or she must be wise, possess intelligence (*phronēsis*), and show self-control (*enkrateia*), which, as the letter of Aristeas (221–22) indicates, means not to set out for new territories and glory. A king should avoid laziness, excess, and hedonistic behavior.

The monarch must demonstrate *praotēs* in reproving those at fault, as we saw in the case of Isocrates' advice *To Nicocles*[29] by "making the punishment less than the offense." This trait may take on an aspect of forbearance: in his later life Plutarch reports that Alexander showed remorse over the razing of Thebes. Memory of the event often caused him grief "and made him *praoteron* toward many people."[30] The defeated Cleopatra tells Augustus that she had held back from her treasures some small gifts for Octavia and Livia, in order that through their intercession she would find her conqueror "gracious and *praoteron*."[31] *Praotēs* here is the product of conscious effort rather than a spontaneous reaction. Plutarch is equally clear that although *praotēs* is a matter of training, a person cannot develop it without a natural inclination to it. In describing the reasons for the political impotence of Agesipolis, the coruler of King Agesilaus, whose stronger will he follows, Plutarch lists the exile of his father, his youth, and his natural character.[32] Agesipolis has not developed his natural temperament, which is that

---

26. Walbank, "Monarchies," 83.
27. *Ep. Arist.* 265.
28. Xenophon *Agesilaus* 11.5–6.
29. Introduction, p. 5 above.
30. Plutarch *Alexander* 13. The form *praoteron* is the comparative.
31. Plutarch *Anthony* 83.6. Hubert Martin Jr., "The Concept of *Praotēs* in Plutarch's *Lives*," *Greek, Roman, and Byzantine Studies* 3 (1960): 65–73; for a general discussion see Jacqueline de Romilly, *La douceur dans la pensée grecque* (Paris: Société d'Édition, "Les Belles Lettres," 1979).
32. *Phusei de praos kai kosmios.* Plutarch *Agesilaus* 20.7.

of self-restraint. In short, a Hellenistic monarch must be someone of the highest moral stature. Most seem to have exercised patronage by functioning somewhere between love of glory and common bribery.[33]

Ruler Cults

A ruler cult is a form of worship offered to a monarch. It might involve the identification of a ruler with a particular god. While a distinction between honoring a superior person and worshiping a god might seem obvious to us, in the Hellenistic world there were subtle and minute distinctions that even the sources do not entirely clarify. Some of these distinctions rely on the permeable boundaries between humans and gods. While some strands of Greek thought rejected any blending of distinctions between the gods and the human race, other strands were not so clear.

Whether a ruler was granted a cult statue for worship or simply an image would be one example of a distinction in status. A ruler cult may be connected to the veneration of heroes for their glorious activities perhaps on the field of battle or as the founder of a city. Impetus for worship comes spontaneously from a monarch's subjects.

Even before Alexander, various generals and kings were granted divine honors sporadically. In Macedonia there is evidence of cults of Amyntas III at Pydna and Philip II at Amphipolis. On the day of his death at Aegae, Philip arranged for his statue to be carried along with those of the twelve gods, perhaps more for homage rather than worship. Radical change in the ruler cult came with Alexander.

During his lifetime, some Greek cities in Asia Minor established ruler cults. It is hard to date their provenance, but one could reasonably assume after liberation from Persia in 334/3. In 323/4, Alexander requested divine honors from the Greeks of Europe. At Athens, cults for both him and Hephaestion were established, but this and any others did not outlast his death. However, the precedent had been established, and within the next few decades cults were being set up all over the Greek world in honor of the

---

33. Klaus Bringmann, "The King as Benefactor: Some Remarks on Ideal Kingship in the Age of Hellenism," in *Images and Ideologies: Self-Definition in the Hellenistic World*, ed. Anthony Bullock, Erich S. Gruen, A. A. Long, and Andrew Stewart (Berkeley: University of California Press, 1993), 7–24.

new rulers. In 307 Antigonus and his son Demetrius were worshiped as saviors at Athens after Demetrius's liberation of the city.
In 290 the text of a hymn was recorded by Duris of Samos, part
of which reads:

> O son of the most mighty god Poseidon and of Aphrodite,
> hail! For other gods are either far away or have not ears, or
> do not exist or heed us not at all; but thee we can see in very
> presence, not in word and not in stone but in truth. And so
> we pray to thee.[34]

The hymn reflects the attitude that led to ruler-worship and confirms that such a cult was not part of the routine of flattery to
royals.

The practice continued and grew in the Roman empire. At its
heart lay the sacrifice, performed by cult officials, normally of an
animal but sometimes incense and libations performed on a defi-
nite day, either monthly, yearly, or in every fourth year. It might
be combined with the festival of a god or held on the birthday of
the monarch or the day commemorating the particular event connected with the establishment of the cult/altar. At the festival there
would be competitions of various kinds and a procession accompanied by singing. Sometimes a month was named after the monarch.
Those so honored often had epithets connected to the circumstances giving rise to the cult. Thus the same king might be greeted
by different titles in different cities. Perhaps a title conferred by a
city in the course of a special cult, such as *Sōtēr* (Savior), which
was used of Ptolemy at Rhodes, was a forerunner of an official dynastic title. Although the Roman emperor Augustus usually refused
worship of himself as a deity, it was acceptable to recognize and
venerate a divine presence that explained his extraordinary success
and power. Augustus himself held the position of *pontifex max-
imus* (high priest) and the title *divi filius* (son of a god). As high
priest he mediated between humanity and the gods, and as son of
a god (or son of a divinity — the distinction is negligible) he had a
quasi-divine status.

Because the ruler cult originates in an act of special benefit, it
celebrates gifts of the monarch rather than qualities. Thus the ruler
does what the god is expected to do. Aristotle records that honor
is a recognition of a good reputation for benefactions and that
honors consist of sacrifices, privileges, sacred enclosures, the right

---

34. Cited in Walbank, "Monarchies," 91.

to front seats, tombs, images, meals at public expense, barbarian honors like *proskunēsis* (prostration) and keeping at a distance, and gifts.[35] While these are all afforded to humans, in the cult itself there is room for ambiguity as to the recipient of the sacrifice. A Latin inscription of C.E. 11 on a marble altar at Narbo (modern-day Narbonne in France) prays to the Roman emperor Caesar Augustus and his divine spirit.[36] We shall shortly see that opposition to the ruler cult is not to the thing itself but rather that the recipient is unworthy. The ruler cult will not go away.

Prostration and Alexander

What we learn about the act of *proskunēsis* (prostration or obeisance) to Alexander derives from several sources about his life. It is an important facet of the Hellenistic notion of kingship since it reflects veneration of a human as if he were a god. After Alexander, it is an implicit part of the cult of monarchy. Its use varies from place to place.

In one incident, possibly an eyewitness account, Diodorus reports that late in 333 on the morning after the battle of the Issus, Alexander and Hephaestion paid a visit to Darius's mother, Sisygambris, his wife, and his children, who had been left behind as the Persian army fled:

> The two men were both dressed alike, but Hephaestion was taller and more handsome. Sisygambris took him for the king and prostrated (*proskunein*) herself before him. The others present signaled to her and pointed to Alexander; embarrassed at her own ignorance, she began to prostrate herself again, before Alexander this time, but he cut in and said, "Never mind, mother; for he is Alexander too." By thus addressing the old woman as "Mother," with this most beneficent of salutations he signaled to those unlucky women the benefactions that were to come.[37]

This fascinating anecdote, appearing in other accounts of Alexander's life,[38] introduces some key issues in his (and the sources')

---

35. Aristotle *Rh.* 1.5 1361A 28–32.
36. Dan Schowalter, "Written in Stone: A Prayer to Augustus," in *Prayer from Alexander to Constantine: A Critical Anthology,* ed. Mark Kiley (London and New York: Routledge, 1997), 159–64.
37. Diodorus *Histories* 17.37.5–6.
38. Plutarch *Alexander* 21; Arrian *Anabasis of Alexander* 2.12.3–8.

attitude to kingship: the tension between the reality of Alexander's appearance and the expectations of kingly demeanor; the attachment to Hephaestion; the connection between his self-mastery, his charisma, and his power over others; the tension between his role as Macedonian monarch and king of Asia and the strangeness of the practice of *proskunēsis* to the Greek. It indicates too the role of *philanthrōpia* in Alexander's conception of his own mission.

From Plutarch's *Alexander* we learn that the topic was controversial. When Alexander decided in 327 to enforce the Persian custom of *proskunēsis* into court ceremonial, Kallisthenes, a friend and a philosopher traveling with Alexander, refused to comply because, he argued, the Greeks did this only before the gods. Plutarch reports the verdict of Aristotle on Kallisthenes: he showed great ability as a speaker but lacked common sense.[39] Over the issue of *proskunēsis,* by refusing to perform the act and instead rehearsing in public the reasons for objecting, he articulated what the Macedonians secretly thought, and although he saved Alexander from insisting upon compliance, he destroyed himself, seeming to use force rather than persuasion with the king.[40] After Alexander's death, prostration became natural and necessary.

We must say something about the perspective of the sources themselves. Plutarch wrote his life of Alexander around C.E. 110–15 under the emperor Trajan. It is paired with his life of Caesar. Although the essay comparing the two men is now lost, Plutarch saw his task as essentially didactic. With the ultimate aim of revealing character he uses many different sources while anecdotes illustrate examples of virtues and vice.

Plutarch's selection begins with Alexander's genealogy indicating greatness through Herakles on his father's side and Achilles on his mother's. Countering a prevalent idea that power corrupts a king, he presents Alexander as moderate and self-controlled. Elsewhere Plutarch maintains that while Alexander believed in his divine parentage, he was properly circumspect about it, using it only to secure his power.[41] Not irrelevant to his project is the interest of the emperor in Plutarch's subject matter.

An important factor in Alexander's latent power is his continence. After a defeat of the Persians at Issus, the wife, mother, and two unmarried daughters of Darius are found left behind in the

---

39. Plutarch *Alexander* 54 (695).
40. Ibid. (695–96).
41. Ibid., 28 (681).

Persian camp. Learning of this, Alexander sends word to them that Darius was not dead and that they were not to be afraid for themselves since they should have everything they used to think their due when Darius was king. Plutarch observes that if this message was thought by the women to be *praos* and kindly, Alexander's actions proved even more humane. "Alexander, as it would seem, considering the mastery of himself a more kingly thing than the conquest of his enemies, neither laid hands on these women, nor did he know any other before marriage."[42]

The tension between praise and censure of Alexander, less visible in the laudatory works of Plutarch, is overt in the writings of Arrian. A Bithynian, Roman senator, and governor of Cappadocia, he wrote an account called the *Anabasis of Alexander*. Recognizing Alexander's vices, anger, and drunkenness, he nevertheless praises Alexander for repenting of rash action. Alexander's claim to be son of Zeus he excuses as "a device to make him more impressive to his subjects."[43] On the question of *proskunēsis,* Arrian is straightforward:

> The fact is that the report prevails that Alexander wanted people actually to prostrate (*proskuneisthai*) themselves before him, from the underlying idea that his father was Ammon and not Philip, and as he was now expressing his admiration for the ways of the Persians and Medes, both in his change of dress and in addition by the alteration in his court etiquette.[44]

Arrian's Alexander is cast in the mold of Arrian's contemporaries, the emperors Trajan, Hadrian, and Antoninus Pius: a man at the apex of human good fortune, distinguished by his generally moderate use of power, able to admit his faults, and probably divinely conceived. Since moral criticism is fundamentally incompatible with an encomium, in the latter part of his work he seems to struggle uneasily.

Both Plutarch and Arrian allude to the parallels between Alexander's deeds and those of the hero of the *Iliad,* Achilles. Plutarch links the heroes implicitly, but Arrian is explicit. He mentions Achilles twice: once at the celebrated visit to Achilles' tomb at Troy and once when Alexander is mourning for Hephaestion. According to Plutarch, Alexander carries Aristotle's recension of the

---

42. Ibid., 21 (676).
43. Arrian *Anabasis* 7.29.3.
44. Ibid., 4.9.9.

Iliad with him into Asia. Like Achilles, Alexander abstains from sex and sleep. He sulks in his tent when he is thwarted, and his relationship with Hephaestion mirrors that of Achilles with Patroklos. Yet Plutarch introduces qualities that Alexander demonstrates never once thought important to the earlier heroic age: *praotēs, sōphrosunē* (self-control),[45] and *philanthrōpia*. Plutarch is clear about Alexander's nature from adolescence: "being contentious not to be forced but being easily led by reason to duty."[46] As in the question of *proskunēsis*, so in Alexander's nature persuasion replaces force as the overriding motivation for conduct. Traits such as these are not found in the pages of Homer.

In another essay entitled *On the Fortune or the Virtue of Alexander*, Plutarch asks, as the title implies, whether fortune or excellence was primarily responsible for Alexander's success. In the previous essay, *On the Fortune of the Romans*, Plutarch points out that the Romans achieved world unity because fortune put fewer obstacles in their path. By contrast, fortune hampered and finally killed Alexander. In fact, according to Plutarch, Alexander displays many virtues. In an extended discussion toward the end of the essay, Plutarch opines that everything he did is the product of the virtues courage, justice, self-control, and *praotēs* rather than of the caprice of fortune or the violence of war. Courage, justice, and wisdom are three of the four traditional cardinal virtues. That *praotēs* has been added to it and become part of the fourfold canon is remarkable. But what is distinctive about Alexander is the tempering of his competitive virtues with the quiet ones:

> One sees that in Alexander the warlike is also humane, the *praon* also manly, the liberal provident, the irascible placable, the amatory temperate, his relaxation not idle, and his labors not without recreation. Who but he combined festivals with wars, campaigns with revels, Bacchic rites and weddings and nuptial songs with sieges and battle fields? Who was ever more hostile to wrongdoers or kinder to the unfortunate? Who more stern to his opponents or more indulgent to petitioners?[47]

And so the figure who gave the Hellenistic age its name, whose short life full of military successes traces out its geographical con-

---

45. Plutarch *Alexander* 4.
46. Ibid., 7.
47. Plutarch *On the Fortune of Alexander* 332C–D.

tours, becomes for Plutarch one who embodies in his life and deeds the merit of the quiet as well as the competitive virtues.

The Hellenistic Court of Herod the Great

At the heart of the Hellenistic monarchy, large and conspicuous royal palaces and monuments were constructed.[48] The court was the primary zone of influence by means of which Hellenistic kings consolidated their reigns. Eventually bureaucracies developed to administer territories. These were rudimentary at first, revolving around a few individuals with different duties: treasurer, and scribe, for example. But within the court the power structure was centralized in the monarch. Around him (or her) were groups of royal supporters. These were called the friends (*philoi*). By means of the friends, Hellenistic kings created a ruling class. The *philoi* at all Hellenistic courts were Greek and Macedonian; there were virtually no natives among them. Occasionally Persians and other non-Greeks found their way into courts but not in large numbers. They were given prestige, power, lands, and money. Over time their positions became hereditary. Sometimes *philoi* were personal friends of the king. Honored *philoi* appear in the literature. With the Ptolemies, a single "kinsman" (*suggenēs*) formed the head of the court hierarchy who might be designated "brother" or even "father and brother" by the king. Through the court, the influence of the monarch reached subjects of the realm. The king's birthday was a public festival, his death an occasion for public mourning; dating was usually by the years of a reign, and the monarch's portraits adorned the coins.

In comparison with the growing bureaucracies of the Ptolemies at Alexandria and the Seleucids at Antioch, the Antigonid court at Pella was simple. There were no real helpers in the business of government. The Attalids constructed a new and imposing court at Pergamon. Outside the central palace, every kingdom had palaces elsewhere. The Seleucids had palaces at Sardes, Seleucia on the Tigris, Susa, Mopsuestia, and Gabae. Herod the Great, a Roman client king, built palaces within his realm that he visited at different seasons.

Matthew's Gospel, to which we will shortly turn, briefly describes Herod the Great and his court. We are fortunate to have

---

48. Inge Nielsen, *Hellenistic Palaces: Tradition and Renewal*, Studies in Hellenistic Civilization 5 (Aarhus: Aarhus University Press, 1994).

another account of Herod and his court from Josephus. This account makes it clear that Herod, like the Hasmoneans, resembled the Hellenistic monarch.[49] Before we turn to Josephus, let us review evidence for a Hasmonean concept of kingship.[50]

First, there is the evidence of the Temple Scroll from Qumran, which can be dated no more specifically than to the Hasmonean period.[51] In it, Deuteronomy 17:14–20 is given prominence and partly reinterpreted. The king is to have only one wife, and an army of twelve thousand (derived from Numbers 31:4) to be mobilized differently according to rank.[52] Although the scroll criticizes a Hasmonean ruler, none can be identified specifically.

Next is the evidence of Sirach, dated after 132 B.C.E. It recapitulates God's empowerment of David. On account of his military victories, David was offered "a diadem of glory," and his kingship was given by way of covenant.[53] However, with Simon, the high priest becomes the preeminent religious and political leader of the nation. Ben Sirach eulogizes Simon in 50:1–21. Although there was no monarchy, the role of high priest here has a political as well as a cultic dimension. With Simon's high priesthood and rule together with that of the other Hasmoneans comes a display of Judean autonomy. The same blending of priestly and kingly roles may be seen in the vision of Judas Maccabeus of the high priest Onias just before battle:

> What he saw was this: Onias, who had been high priest, a noble and good man, of modest bearing and *praon de ton tropon*,[54] one who spoke fittingly and had been trained from childhood in all that belongs to excellence, was praying with outstretched hands for the whole body of the Jews.[55]

Josephus's *Antiquities of the Jews*, written in Rome in the later first century C.E., is the only surviving history of any Near Eastern people to link their past in the ancient orient with their present

---

49. Victor Tcherikover, *Hellenistic Civilization and the Jews*, trans. S. Applebaum (New York: Athenaeum, 1970), 253.

50. Tessa Rajak, "Hasmonean Kingship and the Invention of Tradition," in *Aspects of Hellenistic Kingship*, ed. Per Bilde, Troels Engberg-Pedersen, Lise Hannestad, and Jan Zahle, Studies in Hellenistic Civilization 7 (Oakville, Conn.: Aarhus University Press, 1996), 99–115.

51. Geza Vermes, ed. and trans., *The Complete Dead Sea Scrolls in English* (London and New York: Penguin, 1997), 190–219.

52. 11QT57.

53. Sirach 47:6, 13.

54. I would like to translate this "meek with respect to bearing."

55. 2 Maccabees 15:12.

under Roman rule.[56] Josephus describes Herod, the son of Antipater, as "of no more than a vulgar family, and of no eminent extraction, but one that was subject to other kings."[57] As far as kingly qualities are concerned, Herod feigns them. He pretends to be forgiving to his family on account of his *megalopsuchia* and his great moderation (*epieikeia*) when in fact he is determined to kill the offending persons.[58] He has his successor and high priest Hyrcanus killed on a trumped-up charge. Hyrcanus, in contrast to Herod, has a mild (*epieikēs*) and moderate (*metrios*) disposition. To the powerful Romans, Herod is conciliatory. Josephus tells us that he set off to meet the victorious Octavian (the future Augustus) after the battle of Actium on the island of Rhodes in 30 B.C.E. Laying aside his royal diadem in submission, Herod argues that his loyalty to Antony should be construed as a sign of his prospective loyalty to Octavian. Octavian assents and confirms Herod as king.[59] Josephus describes Herod's conduct as one of *megalopsuchia*.

> [Herod] also desired that Caesar would not put to death one Alexander, who had been a companion of Anthony; but Caesar had sworn to put him to death, and so he could not obtain his petition; and now he returned to Judea again with greater honor and assurance than ever and affrighted those that had expectations to the contrary, as still acquiring from his very dangers greater splendor than before, by the favor of God to him.[60]

Herod escorts Octavian on his way to Egypt through Syria, entertains him lavishly at Ptolemais, and provides supplies for the crossing of the desert. On Octavian's return after the conquest of Egypt, he escorts him as far north as Antioch. In between he goes to see Octavian in Egypt and receives for his pains additions to his kingdom in the form of Hippos on the eastern shore of the Sea of Galilee; Gadara beyond the Jordan; Jericho in the Jordan Valley; Samaria; and a line of small places on the coast, including Joppa, Gaza, and Strato's Tower. In all this he proves himself to be a most worthy friend of Caesar.

---

56. Fergus Millar, *The Roman Near East: 31 B.C.–A.D. 337* (Cambridge, Mass.: Harvard University Press, 1993), 5.
57. Josephus *Ant.* 14.4.491.
58. Ibid., 15.3.48.
59. Josephus *J.W.* 1.20.1–3 (386–93); *Ant.* 15 6.6–7 (187–93).
60. Josephus *Ant.* 15.7.197–98.

Here we see clearly the power structure defining the status of Herod as a client king of the Romans. Octavian operates by personal conduct and giving of favors, arbitrarily transferring places and cities from Roman rule to royal control or vice versa in the case of Zeugma. Octavian marches forces through royal territory and back, just as Herod escorts him through Syria.

Meanwhile, between visits to the Roman emperor, on the home front all is not well for Herod. His wife Mariamne receives news of his success with open hatred. Toward her Herod vacillates between affection and anger:

> But by always changing one passion for another he was still in real uncertainty, and thus was entangled between hatred and love, and was frequently disposed to inflict punishment on her for her insolence toward him; but being deeply in love with her in his soul, he was not able to dispense with her.[61]

Just at the point when ill passions were more and more inflamed on both sides, Herod hears the news of Caesar's victory at Actium and distractedly leaves. Josephus presents a king whose external demeanor is not consonant with his personal life. He is given to frequent outbursts of anger. Such irrational behavior has its consequences: at the trial and eventual sentencing of Mariamne, "Herod kept no temper in what he said, and was in too great a passion for judging well about the matter."[62] After her death, he wanders off into desert places, ostensibly hunting, but in fact physically and mentally ill. This is the opposite of the bearing of a Hellenistic king whose self-control matches ability to rule.

Mariamne for her part treats her husband imperiously, according to Josephus. She fails to take into account that she lives under a monarchy and is at another's disposal. This conflict between appearance and reality shows that while Herod looks like a Hellenistic king from the outside, he is not one on the inside. We cannot assume that the external appearance is all that matters. External appearance and internal reality go together. Josephus explains that as much external success as Herod achieves, so much the greater were the difficulties of his household.[63]

After several years, when Herod restores equanimity to his household by having several members dispatched, Josephus describes Herod's attempts to remove the ill opinion subjects had of

---

61. Ibid., 15.7.211–12.
62. Ibid., 15.7.229.
63. Ibid., 15.7.218.

him by liberally dispensing care and *megalopsuchia* toward them.[64] Yet this is not genuine. He still fortifies his cities and provides security for the government to secure his kingdom. The inhabitants of Gadara, after seventeen years of Herod's rule, complain of Herod's heavy and tyrannical injunctions to Caesar Augustus when he visits Syria in 20 B.C.E.[65] And yet Herod exerts influence over the Jews of the diaspora as monarch of Israel.

The life of the Hasmonean court was fashioned on the model of the court life of the Hellenistic monarchies[66] even while they appealed to the specific traditions about kings in the Hebrew Bible. The same is true of Herod. After he became king, Herod did not forget that the Jewish council of elders threatened his life ten years earlier after his attempts to claim to the Gentile territories in Galilee and had subsequently supported his enemy Antigonus, one of the Hasmoneans. Forty-five of its seventy-one members were executed, and the council was deprived of all its political power and superseded by a private council of Herod's *philoi*. Members of his court would have included the king's extended family, bodyguards, and the court friends. Among them was the historian Nicolaus of Damascus, who supplies Josephus with information. From the pages of Josephus, Nicolaus's speech before Marcus Agrippa (the representative of Augustus) defending the right of Asian Jews not to appear in court on the sabbath is preserved. In all likelihood this speech is quite authentic. Agrippa is persuaded.

Intellectuals like Nicolaus might be permanent or temporary attachments to the court. To cater to the needs of all these people, there would be physicians, scribes, secretaries, bakers, attendants, and many specialist and nonspecialist slaves. The more powerful *philoi* would have their families present together with individual followers. Presumably there would be factions among the *philoi* depending on political issues and circumstances of the moment. Josephus speaks specifically about Herod's court etiquette:

> If anyone was not very obsequious to [Herod] in his language and would not confess himself to be his slave, or even seem to think of any innovation in his government, he was not able

---

64. Ibid., 15.8.326.
65. Ibid., 15.10.354. Cf. 16.1.4: "He did not act as a king but as a tyrant."
66. Tcherikover, *Hellenistic Civilization*, 252. For a general discussion, see Gabriel Herman, "The Court Society of the Hellenistic Age," in *Hellenistic Constructs: Essays in Culture, History, and Historiography*, ed. Peter Cartledge, Peter Garnsey, and Eric S. Gruen (Berkeley: University of California Press, 1997), 199–224.

to contain himself, but prosecuted his kin and friends, and punished them as if they were enemies; and this wickedness he undertook out of a desire that he might be himself alone honored.[67]

Herod's funeral procession in 4 B.C.E. is as ostentatious as that of any Hellenistic king. Members of the procession were probably members of the court. The body is covered in purple with precious stones; a diadem is on the head, and a scepter is in the right hand. About the bier were Herod's sons and numerous relations, followed by the army ranks, followed by five hundred domestics carrying spices.

Conclusion

In the course of this chapter, I have surveyed some facets of Hellenistic monarchy from Alexander to the first century of the common era. The Romans had a deep distrust of monarchy, and in their earliest contacts with Hellenistic kings, senators and other Romans found them curious and strange and treated them with suspicion. The famous meeting between C. Popillius Laenas and Antiochus IV at Eleusis near Alexandria, at which Antiochus was ostentatiously humbled in front of his *philoi,* was intended as a demonstration of the power now exercised by the republic over kings.[68] By the first century, kings were pawns in Roman politics. However, as we saw from the prayer to Augustus in Gaul, the legacy of Hellenistic kingship lived on in the Roman republic and in one particular corner of that republic in the first century C.E. It reemerged in the Holy Roman Empire and medieval Europe.

---

67. Josephus *Ant.* 16.5.156.
68. Polybius 29.27.1–7.

Chapter 4

JESUS THE MEEK KING
IN MATTHEW'S GOSPEL

There are two passages in which Jesus is described as having several virtues in Matthew's Gospel. In one of them he is clearly a king. In the first passage, Jesus says:

Come to me, all who labor and are heavy laden, and I will give you rest. Take my yoke upon you, and learn from me; for I am *praus* and lowly in heart, and you will find rest for your souls.[1]

Later in the narrative, as Jesus enters Jerusalem, Matthew reports:

This took place to fulfill what was spoken by the prophet, saying, "Tell the daughter of Zion, Behold, your king is coming to you, *praus,* and mounted on an ass, and on a colt, the foal of an ass."[2]

In this chapter I argue that Matthew's Gospel presents Jesus as a *praus* king who in accordance with Jewish tradition is God's son. Jesus' self-description is that of a Hellenistic ruler. While this is self-evident for Matthew 21:5, it has to be argued in the case of Matthew 11:29–30.

First, one has to explain the kind of Judaism that Matthew's Gospel represents: the reaffirmation of a sectarian Judaism at home in the larger cultural world of the Mediterranean.[3] For the Hellenistic world as a whole Hellenism and Judaism are by no means

---

1. Matthew 11:28–29.
2. Matthew 21:4–5. I am deferring a discussion of "the meek" in Matthew 5:5 until chapter 5.
3. Erich S. Gruen, "Fact and Fiction: Jewish Legends in a Hellenistic Context," in *Hellenistic Constructs: Essays in Culture, History, and Historiography,* ed. Peter Cartledge, Peter Garnsey, and Erich S. Gruen (Berkeley: University of California Press, 1997), 72–88. See also A. J. Saldarini, *Pharisees, Scribes, and Sadducees in Palestinian Society: A Sociological Approach* (Wilmington, Del.: Glazier, 1988).

antithetical, although it is hard to say exactly how far Greek culture permeated Palestine in the Hellenistic period. Matthew represents a recasting of Greek traditions to conform to the language and Scriptures of Judaism. When Matthew describes Jesus as a *praus* king in 21:5, he is quoting from Zechariah.

The presentation of Jesus as a *praus* king not only in Matthew 21:5 but also in the earlier passage, 11:27–30, is not widely recognized. Many scholars do recognize that motifs of kingship resound through the Gospel. But very few connect kingship with virtues. While most scholars recognize that behind 11:27–30 is the question of Jesus' identity, the same scholars label Jesus in the passage as either Wisdom, or Teacher, or Son, or Servant of God, or authoritative Revealer, or a combination of two or three titles.[4] To my mind, it is important to hold the question of identity together with the virtues of that figure.

The warrant for seeing Jesus as Wisdom began with the work of David F. Strauss, who saw connections between the passage and Sirach 51.[5] Most influential since Strauss has been M. Jack Suggs, who argued that in Matthew Jesus is not merely a wisdom teacher but Wisdom (Sophia).[6] Connections with Sirach 51 are made through the words "toil" and "yoke" and the verb "to find rest":

> Put your neck under the yoke, and let your souls receive instruction; it is to be found close by. See with your eyes that I have labored little and found myself much rest.[7]

Here, however, there is not much toil going on, no reference to "those who labor and are heavy-laden," and no description of the qualities of Wisdom in Sirach. Ben Sirach knows very well what the word means. He counsels a prominent individual to perform tasks with *prautēs* since "the greater you are, the more you must

---

4. Celia Deutsch, *Hidden Wisdom and the Easy Yoke: Wisdom, Torah, and Discipleship in Matthew 11:25–30* (Sheffield: Sheffield Academic Press, 1987), 44; idem, "Jesus-Wisdom the Teacher," in *Lady Wisdom, Jesus, and the Sages: Metaphor and Social Context in Matthew's Gospel* (Valley Forge, Pa.: Trinity Press International, 1996), 81–110; M. Eugene Boring, "The Gospel of Matthew," in *The New Interpreter's Bible*, 12 vols. (Nashville: Abingdon, 1994–), 8:275.

5. Hans-Dieter Betz summarizes work on the passage including that of Strauss in "The *Logion* of the Easy Yoke and of Rest," *Journal of Biblical Literature* 86 (1967): 10–24.

6. M. J. Suggs, *Wisdom, Christology, and Law in Matthew's Gospel* (Cambridge, Mass.: Harvard University Press, 1970).

7. Sirach 51:26–27; 43:30 mentions "not growing weary."

humble yourself,"[8] and he describes a *praus* woman as the glory of her husband:

> A woman's beauty gladdens the countenance, and surpasses every human desire. If *prautēs* and humility mark her speech, her husband is not like other men.[9]

These uses of the noun and adjective retain a traditional understanding of gender roles. They have nothing to do with the traits of Wisdom in Sirach. For these reasons, Wisdom traditions are not the immediate source of the descriptions of Jesus in Matthew 11:29. While they are not in the foreground, however, Wisdom traditions lie not far away.

The warrant for identifying Jesus as teacher comes from Jesus' command in the passage to "learn from me." Presumably a teacher described as "*praus* and lowly of heart" would not be a harsh taskmaster. Certainly the speaker of the passage has authority. But I see no compelling reason to assume that the one "*praus* and lowly of heart" must be a teacher other than the general one that Jesus teaches in Matthew's Gospel. One can learn from any person.

The warrant for seeing Jesus as Son and Revealer comes from the preceding verse:

> All things have been delivered to me by my Father; and no one knows the Son except the Father, and no one knows the Father except the Son and anyone to whom the Son chooses to reveal him.[10]

If we clarify the understanding of "Son" then we are closer to seeing the connection between the "son" and the virtues of Matthew 11:29. The son is "*praus* and lowly of heart" because the son is a king. God recognizes Israel's king as son in Psalm 2:7. Matthew's Gospel has an extensive christology of Jesus as Son developed in relation to God as Father from the birth narratives to the baptism (3:17). This would be the first place where virtues of the Son were listed.

The passage obviously speaks of a person in authority. The internal warrant for speaking of Jesus as king in Matthew 11:28–30 is that it explains the yoke of service placed upon followers that is "easy" and the burden that is "light." The connections between

---

8. Sirach 3:17–18.
9. Sirach 36:22–23.
10. Matthew 11:27.

monarchy and servitude are not hard to make. The Romans write on bronze tablets to the Jewish nation, according to 1 Maccabees,

> And concerning the wrongs which King Demetrius is doing to [the Jews] we have written to him as follows, "Why have you made your yoke heavy upon our friends and allies the Jews?"[11]

Graham Stanton proposes that the invitation of 11:28 is spoken by Jesus as the humble Servant of God. He interprets the humility of Jesus in relation to the role of Jesus as a servant at 12:15, where Matthew describes Jesus' fulfillment of Isaiah 42:1 and Jesus' healing ministry, which Matthew sees as fulfilling Isaiah 53:4: "He took away our illnesses and lifted our diseases from us" (8:17).[12] Stanton's criticism of Suggs is helpful. While his suggestion about the identity of Jesus as Servant has merit, it passes over the role of king in 21:5 and neglects the role of the Son in 11:27. My interpretation differs only in emphasis by including the virtues in the search for identity. *Praus* makes most sense of the context of Son as king.

Over a century ago, some scholars went to the other extreme, recognizing the importance of Greek material for the understanding of the term "meek" in Matthew's Gospel but not looking specifically at Hellenistic texts or at Hellenistic ideas about monarchy. These discussions refer to Matthew 5:5, "Blessed are the *praeis,* for theirs is the kingdom of heaven."

Pre-Twentieth Century Scholarship

The American scholar William Porcher Du Bose, writing at the beginning of the twentieth century, maintains that the meekness spoken of in Matthew 5:5 is "the universal attitude of Jesus Christ, and so the essential Christian attitude in all the personal relations of men, and under all circumstances of possible provocation or trial or temptation."[13] Du Bose's comments were widely read. His book and in particular his observations on the meekness of Jesus and its connection to Greek thought were the objects of special admiration by the Lady Margaret Professor of Christ Church Oxford,

---

11. 1 Maccabees 8:31.

12. Graham Stanton, "Matthew 11:28–30: Comfortable Words?" in *A Gospel for a New People: Studies in Matthew* (Edinburgh: T. & T. Clark, 1992), 364–77.

13. William Porcher Du Bose, *The Gospel in the Gospels* (London: Longmans, Green and Co., 1906), 102.

William Sanday, who took the passage as a good average sample of the freshness and originality with which Du Bose writes. Sanday commends Du Bose as a philosophic theologian[14] and even the wisest Anglican writer.[15]

Du Bose maintains that the Beatitudes will illustrate "the gospel of the common humanity and the earthly life of our Lord" since blessedness is both the highest reach and attainment of that life.[16] Using Aristotle's idea of pleasure completing a function in two aspects to speak of blessedness, namely, that it is the completion and that it causes the completion, Jesus in saying "Blessed are the meek, for they will inherit the earth" describes his own life and "the life that should be ours in its very fullness and completion. . . . The beatitudes are the revelation of His own humanly discovered and humanly experienced secret of blessedness."[17] For example, Jesus knew the poverty that is the condition of the kingdom of heaven, the sorrow without which one cannot experience the divine consolations, and the meekness through which he was to inherit the earth. He, too, had hungered and thirsted for righteousness and been filled; through the purity of his human heart he had seen God . . . and had tested what it was not only to be called but to be the Son of God.

The beatitude "Blessed are the meek" thus illustrates the life and character of Christ. It reflects the disposition of "men towards men" that is ultimately true and essential and that will in the end inherit the earth. Du Bose observes how curious it is that "in all the great answers to the question of human relationship and conduct, the same term has been selected to express the ideal" while at the same time the inadequacy of the term has been felt and expressed.[18] Aristotle calls the disposition of men to one another meekness, mildness, or gentleness, but, according to Du Bose, laments that the term is not positive or strong enough. Likewise, he argues, we have all felt the inadequacy of the term "meekness" to describe the character or disposition of Moses. And yet our Lord selected the same term to express his fundamental disposition. Du Bose laments

14. William Sanday, *The Life of Christ in Recent Research* (New York: Oxford University Press, 1907), 266.

15. Ibid., 281.

16. Du Bose, *The Gospel in the Gospels*, 86.

17. Ibid., 87. In deference to the source, which itself reflects the piety of the period, I have matched the tone and language in the material that follows.

18. Ibid., 99.

the term's negative and colorless quality. After all, it expresses his great principle of nonresistance.

The Greek idea of meekness rests upon the idea of reasonableness and moderation, self-control, and freedom of the will from prejudice and passion. These qualities express the intellectual and moral conditions of the ideal temper.[19] Lacking, however, was what Paul calls "the things of the other." Thus Jesus realizes in himself the full manifestation of the attitude of meekness toward men under adverse conditions. The temptations of greatness and power shown to him by the devil had no hold on him. All pride, ambition, and self-glorification were dismissed. Only one attitude mattered: to be not Lord but servant of all. To be sure, we have no abstract definition of the term in Matthew. All we have is the manifestation of the term in the life of Jesus. This quality of personal relations is essentially love. This attitude is one that will survive and possess the earth. In the history of our Lord's own kingdom on earth, in spite of our unchristian want of faith and devotion, lies the vindication of his promise.

Du Bose goes on to ask whether the principle of nonresistance is feasible. It must be qualified by common sense and particular circumstances. Taking account of the other by resisting the evildoer might thus be fulfilling the spirit but not the letter of the law. To exercise it we must use reason and judgment.[20]

While it is helpful to find a scholar who explores the virtue of meekness, several traits now seem part of an older perspective. First is the idea that Christianity supersedes Greek thought. Next is the reading of the Gospels through the lens of Paul: the meekness of Matthew's Gospel is best seen as "the love that never faileth...that can be all things yet always the same thing."[21] Next is the self-imposed confinement to classical rather than Hellenistic texts. Finally, Du Bose seems interested only in the virtue itself rather than the context in which it appears.

For Du Bose, Aristotle feels the inadequacy of the term when using it to describe the conduct between humans. This may also be felt, Du Bose argues, in applying the term to Moses. Furthermore, it has contributed to the "too negative and colorless interpretation of Jesus' great principle of nonresistance."[22] What Aristotle says in the *Nicomachean Ethics,* if this is the passage to which Du Bose

19. Ibid., 100–101.
20. Ibid., 104.
21. Ibid., 102.
22. Ibid., 100.

refers (there are no footnotes in the book), is that the intermediate stage *praotēs* represents in regard to the extreme stage of anger in interpersonal contact has no name.[23] This is not the same thing as saying that Aristotle feels the term to be inadequate. Aristotle is defining a state, not a name. Aristotle clarifies that it is hard to define the intermediate stage for several reasons, one of which is that it is easier to deal with the extremes since they occur more frequently. Another is the contingent nature of the situation in which humans function and our perception of that situation; for how long and with whom and for what reasons a person might become justifiably angry before incurring censure are all variables defying exact classification. About all that is clear is that Aristotle commends the intermediate state of *praotēs*. Rather than seeing Aristotle's description of this state as deficient, we can see his account is an attempt to explain the exercise of the median as complex and contingent.

About a century before Du Bose, the 1803 Bampton lectures in Oxford were given by John Farrer, a rector of the united parishes of St. Clement Eastcheap and St. Clement Ongars in London. His subject was the mission and character of Christ and the Beatitudes.[24] He devotes the tenth sermon to Matthew 5:5, "Blessed are the meek, for they shall inherit the earth." As it explores the parameters of the term in some detail, especially in relation to Greek ideas and in light of Jesus' ministry, it is worth quoting at some length.

First, Farrer distinguishes between "the poor" of Matthew 5:3 and "the meek" of Matthew 5:5. The former he understands in reference to God and the things of heaven, while "the meek" he understands with reference to things of earth. Yet the two beatitudes are parallel in structure and hence closely related.

Farrer understands "the meek to be such as are uniformly mild and placid, forbearing and forgiving in their communion with their fellow creatures, such as cultivate an equal mind in the extremes and vicissitudes of life, being content and satisfied in every station, being moderate in prosperity and patient in adversity."[25] These

---

23. Aristotle *Eth. Nic.* 1125B. The translation by Martin Ostwald (London and New York: Macmillan, 1962), renders the term "gentleness," while that of J. A. K. Thompson (Harmondsworth and New York: Penguin, 1955; rev. ed., 1976), translates it as "patience."

24. John Farrer, *Sermons on the Mission and Character of Christ, and on the Beatitudes* (Oxford: Oxford University, 1804).

25. Ibid., 259–60.

qualities he acknowledges to be present in Greek writings (he calls them "Heathen Philosophers") even while its practice was "very feebly cultivated."

The quality of meekness was better taught, Farrer argues, under the dispensation of the Law and commended in the Psalms and the Prophets. Alas! as in the case of the heathen philosophers, it was never practiced even though Moses, the lawgiver himself, exemplifies this quality (here he cites Numbers 12:3). As in the case of Du Bose, the supercessionist approach of Farrer maintains that "it remained for our Lord, a superior teacher of righteousness, to give this quality its proper influence on the heart and practice of mankind."[26]

Jesus exemplifies this quality in the tenor of his own character and conversation. The mildness of his manner we find in the fulfillment of Isaiah 42 cited in Matthew 12:19–20: "He shall not cry aloud nor lift up his voice in the streets. A bruised reed he shall not break, and the dimly burning flax he shall not quench."

In his public ministry he does not come "with a rod of discipline or with the sword of civil power but in peace and love and in the spirit of meekness."[27] He spoke his doctrines in the mildest, easiest, freest manner. In the tone of his preaching "he was gentle, apt to teach, patient; showing all meekness to all men."[28] He did not judge severely those overcome with a sense of sin but "raised them with the language of compassion and consolation." Even to the scribes and Pharisees, he was mild and temperate. When he had occasion to reprehend them "he usually conveyed his sentiments by the circuitous, yet more conciliating mode of parable, rather than by open and direct reproof."[29]

In ordinary dealings with human beings, Jesus forbears and forgives. To the suggestion of vengeance on inhospitable Samaritans made by the disciples he demurs, saying that he was not come to destroy but to save. In the agony of the garden, he submits to the Father's pleasure.[30] On the cross he prays for pardon for those who crucify him (Luke 23:34). Thus he recommends his own disposi-

---

26. Ibid., 261.
27. Ibid., 262.
28. Ibid., 262, with a footnote alluding to 2 Timothy 4:2 and Titus 3:2.
29. Ibid., 262–63.
30. Ibid., 263. "Pleasure" here means that which is in conformity with another's will. This is meaning #2 in the *Oxford English Dictionary (Second Edition) on Compact Disc* (Oxford: Oxford University Press, 1992).

tion as a pattern to his followers: "Learn of me: for I am meek and lowly in heart" (Matt. 11:29).

So too in his doctrine Jesus instructs the disciples in the Sermon on the Mount not to be angry with their brother without cause; to agree with an adversary without delay; neither to resist nor to retaliate evil. Similarly, the apostles Paul (Gal. 5:23) and James (1:21; 3:13) commend to others, from the example of their Lord, this essential spirit of his religion. Peter, "after commending in Christian matrons above all other ornaments the jewel...of a meek and quiet spirit, makes it a general exhortation to Christians, that they be all of one mind, having compassion one of another."[31]

Farrer proposes, as Du Bose would say later, that the character of "the meek" has the same features Paul assigns to charity or Christian love. Here he paraphrases 1 Corinthians 13:4–6. In their personal deportment they are content with their station and condition in life. They are moderate and equal-minded "in both extremes and in all vicissitudes of fortune." In prosperity they turn it to human betterment; in adversity they bow with resignation and are patient under correction.[32]

As in the case of Du Bose, a wholesale appropriation of Farrer does not seem wise. While he is aware of some Greek writings, and he takes more seriously than does Du Bose the example of Moses and the evidence of the Hebrew Scriptures, the tenor of his approach moves the interpretation of the term away from the disciplined benevolence of leaders we have seen in Hellenistic texts (evident in Philo's portrait of Moses, Plutarch's writings, and Josephus's account of the emperor Titus at the siege of Jerusalem) toward the passive disposition of Jesus in his life and death and early Christian emulation of his conduct. The privileging of meekness as patience leads Farrer to an extensive discourse on the benefits the meek can expect in this life since the text under scrutiny promises that the meek shall inherit the earth. Farrer's exposition of the Beatitudes shows that the interpretation of meek as passive has been evident for at least two hundred years. What is helpful is the way Farrer examines the evidence of Jesus' life in Matthew and other Gospels.

The other aspect of *prautēs* to which we must turn before we resume a discussion of Matthew's Gospel is that it is a state of reacting. This is evident in most of the examples of the previous

---

31. Farrer, *Sermons*, 265.
32. Ibid., 267.

chapter: a monarch chooses to be benevolent rather than tyrannical perhaps by freeing prisoners. Aristotle describes *praotēs* as the
mean between anger and no feeling. Since this plays a role in the
interpretation of Matthew, let us explore it further.

Praotēs and Anger

The philosopher Plutarch conducts an extensive exploration of the
quiet virtues. In his treatise *On the Control of Anger*, Sextius Sulla
comments on the change he observes in his friend C. Minicius Fundanus after a year's absence. Virtues already naturally his have
grown, while his impulse to anger "has become so *praon* and
submissive to reason" that the angry impulse itself is much more
mild.[33] As we have seen from Aristotle, evidence of virtues is in
actions. Plutarch marvels that the newly altered Fundanus has not
become indolent, but like the cultivated earth, depths of soil conducive to fruitful action replace previous impetuousness and quick
temper. He inquires how his friend's temper has become so *"praon*
and subservient to reason."[34]

Fundanus embarks on a lengthy explanation. Temper in full
force shuts out sense. One must acquire far in advance, as if one is
expecting a siege, the reinforcements philosophy provides against
temper since in the heat of the storm they are not likely to be
heard. Outbursts of rage may be opposed by judgment. Thus the
soul represses anger and becomes itself firmer and more resistant
to attacks of temper. Even little attacks may be repulsed if one is
silent or pays them no attention. Socrates, feeling himself moved
to too great anger at his friends, "would lower his voice, cause a
smile to spread over his face, and make the expression of his eyes
praoteron," thus establishing within himself a force to counteract
his passion.[35]

Once his cure began, Fundanus observes ire in others. He marvels at the transformation of expression and demeanor it effects.
To reinforce his proposals, Plutarch attacks the value structure that
reinforces anger. He claims that contrary to those who think its
turbulence activity, or its blustering to be confident boldness, or

---

33. Plutarch *De coh. ira* 453B.
34. Ibid., 453C.
35. Ibid., 455B. This is the comparative of *praos*. One would translate something
like "meeker." See also Seneca *De Ira* III.13.3 in Seneca, *Moral Essays* 3 vols., Loeb
Classical Library, ET John W. Basore (Cambridge, Mass.: Harvard University Press,
1928; repr. 1998) 1:286–87.

its obstinacy strength of character and even its cruelty magnificence, its implacability firm resolve and its moroseness hatred of evil, anger is "not well-bred, or manly, nor possessing any quality of pride or greatness."[36] The demeanor of angry persons declares their smallness and weakness not only in their rage against inferiors such as women, children, and animals but also in the slaughter done by tyrants. The weakness of their souls is shown by the strength of their anger.

Plutarch then explains that this correlation of inferiority of soul with extent of wrath is the reason why other weak souls are more prone to anger: women more than men, sick persons more than healthy, old men more than those in their prime, and the unfortunate more than the prosperous. He continues:

> Most prone to anger, for example, are the miser with his steward, the glutton with his cook, the jealous man with his wife, the conceited man when he has been maligned.[37]

Worst of all, he says, are ambitious men too eagerly seeking advancement. From the weakness of such souls comes pain and suffering. From this state arise paroxysms of anger.

The value structure Plutarch opposes views reason and self-containment as signs of weakness leading to inactivity and inertia, expressions of wrath against inferiors as legitimate rights of men in charge of households, retaliation in response to being wronged as legitimate, and those who say that philosophers have no guts. Plutarch advances his argument by identifying tyrants as weak and sick. He also invokes another value system: against those who argue that courage and justice go well together he responds that in the case of retaliation they do not. In this respect, courage fights for possession of *praotēs*[38] alone. Plutarch's value system seeks to replace the courageous and just desire to be avenged on the basis of being wronged with the linking of justice and *praotēs*. To express the desire for revenge is to err "in transferring anger from the women's quarters to the men's." In support of this system, he cites numerous examples of courage and *praotēs* in rulers. Philip of Macedon, Alexander the Great's father, met the hostility of an enemy *philanthropōs*[39] and so transformed his enemy's attitude that he became Philip's eulogist.

---

36. Ibid., 456–57.
37. Ibid., 457B.
38. Ibid., 457D.
39. This is the adverb: "humanely" would be a possible English translation.

Finally, to urge his case, in a discussion of wielding power toward inferiors like servants, Plutarch advocates surrounding power
"with a bulwark of *praotēs*."[40] He cites his own conduct toward
his slaves as an example. While once he treated them harshly, he
finally perceived that it was better to make them worse by forbearance than to "turn against my own self for the correction of
others." He also noted that among the unpunished were those who
were ashamed and so did not repeat the offense. When giving or-
ders in silence rather than using blows, the servants seemed to do
their jobs with enthusiasm. He concludes with his conviction that
"reason is more fit than anger to govern."[41] Beating produces the
kind of wicked intent to do wrong without detection. Patience in
listening to the defense of the accused not only lessens the angry
passion but also avoids the most shameful thing: that the slave
should seem to be making a juster plea than the master.[42] He concludes that the benefit of this merciful, *praos,* and humane spirit is
more beneficial to the one who possesses it than to those brought
into contact with it.

I want to explore next the qualities of *prautēs* that enhance
community life.

A Dispositional Virtue

Contemporary scholars do not agree in assessing the relevance of
Greek material for an understanding of the terms "meek" and
"humble" in Matthew's Gospel. On the one hand, Ulrich Luz proposes that Matthew's use of the term is influenced more by "the
tradition of ecclesiastical interpretation than by Greek usage."[43]
To illustrate the former he cites Gregory of Nyssa's *Homily on
the Beatitudes* and for the latter Aristotle's *Nicomachean Ethics.*
He thinks that Jewish-Christian usage influences Matthew since
the beatitude is a quotation of Psalm 36:11. "The meek" stands
for "poor" (reflecting the Hebrew *anawim),* and the term comes
to mean "humble." This is shown in New Testament passages like
Matthew 11:29, where the terms "meek" and "humble" lie side by
side. Matthew 11:29 includes the element of kindness while 21:5

---

40. Plutarch *De coh. ira* 459C.
41. Ibid., 459D.
42. Ibid., 459E.
43. Ulrich Luz, *Matthew 1–7: A Commentary* (Minneapolis: Augsburg, 1989),
236.

includes the idea of nonviolence. Meekness is thus humility demonstrated in kindness. In Matthew, it is not the renunciation of power or a political strategy of pacifism.[44]

On the other hand, Hans-Dieter Betz states that "there is no question . . . that the [Sermon on the Mount] joins with the Hellenistic world in general when it singles out meekness as a fundamental ethical standard," and he cites in support an array of Greek writers.[45]

Both perspectives relate to what each author thinks of Matthew in general: what sort of writing it is (genre), its environment (milieu), and for whom is it written (audience). For Luz, although Matthew looks like a Hellenistic biography, it is not a typical story of an exemplary human being but the unique story of God with the human Jesus. The Matthean genealogy of chapter 1 and the discourses within the broad context of the story of Jesus suggest rather that the Gospel is a historical proclamation modeled on Mark. Behind the Gospel lie Jewish-Christian partly scribal circles and a worshiping community.[46] This community decided to carry the proclamation of Jesus to the Gentiles. Matthew stands on this threshold in defense of this resolution. The Sermon on the Mount itself is a composition of architectonic symmetry shaped by Matthew himself. At its center is the Lord's Prayer. This ring composition of the sermon stretches into a wider context of the Gospel itself.[47]

For Betz, the Sermon on the Mount is a type of literature called an *epitomē* or "summary," in this case of Jesus' teaching. It was compiled from various oral and written sources in Jewish-Christian circles within one generation of Jesus' death in order to instruct converts from Judaism. The sermon argues for use of the fundamental teachings of Jesus in terms of Jewish theology.[48] Other examples of such "summaries" considered essential within Jewish movements of the time include *The Manual of Discipline* and the

---

44. Ibid. Luz begins his discussion by linking the semantic range of the word to the observation that it becomes a mirror of each interpreter's piety. In this way, the projection of the interpreters supplants the range of interpretations the term conveys. While not denying that interpreters could emphasize aspects of meekness to match their religious outlook, one might ask whether the semantic range of the word does not facilitate this landscape of interpretation.

45. Hans-Dieter Betz, *The Sermon on the Mount*, Hermeneia (Minneapolis: Augsburg Fortress, 1995), 126.

46. Luz, *Matthew*, 77–78.

47. Ibid., 212; diagram, 213.

48. Betz, *Sermon on the Mount*, 73, 80, 88.

Damascus Document from Qumran. From rabbinic Judaism one
may cite the *Pirqe 'Abot* and the *'Abot de Rabbi Nathan*. On the
Greek side there are important literary precursors in Epictetus's
Encheiridion, a handbook compilation of the philosophers' sayings, and its prototype, Epicurus's *Principal Doctrines*. Within the
sermon itself literary evidence such as the functional terms of sense
perception (the use of verbs of seeing and knowing in 5:16 and
6:3), reflection (the use of the verb "to think" in 6:7), and practice
(the use of the verb "to do" in 7:24) point to exercises like those
in Hellenistic philosophy. All these examples intend for the listener
to appropriate an ethical tradition; in the case of the Sermon on
the Mount, for a Jewish listener to hear and put into practice the
teachings of Jesus.

Betz nuances his position carefully. Such philosophical language
as exists within the sermon uses terminology familiar to first-
century Jewish ears. His work relies on a broad understanding of
Jewish movements of the period that have already appropriated
Greek concepts and language. The term "meek," for example, already familiar in Greek ethics, was used by Greek translators of
the Hebrew Bible to interpret the Hebrew word *anawim* (poor) for
Greek-speaking readers. Luz's position is the opposite: the word
"poor" circumscribes the meaning of the Greek word.[49] Betz argues that Matthew understands the virtue of mildness, gentleness,
or meekness as an ethical standard, closely associated with philanthropy and underlying many passages in the Sermon on the
Mount: 5:21–6, 38–42, 43–48; 6:12, 14–15. The opposites of
meekness were brutality and untamed anger. It becomes part of the
description of a Christian sage elsewhere in the New Testament.[50]

A move beyond the alternatives of Luz and Betz is to examine
uses of the Hebrew plural *anawim* (translated poor, humble, or
meek in English) in Jewish sources before or during the first century. Do these texts understand the Hebrew term more narrowly
or more broadly? This would imply some influence from Greek
ideas but not necessarily literary borrowing. We already know that
the term appears in the Hebrew text of Psalm 37:11 and that this
is translated *praeis* in the Greek translation of the Hebrew Scriptures (the Septuagint) at 36:11 and in Matthew's use of it at 5:5.
We know that the same Greek term describes Moses in the Greek
translation of Numbers 12:3. It occurs elsewhere in the Septu-

---

49. Luz, *Matthew*, 236.
50. Betz, *Sermon on the Mount*, 126–27; James 3:13.

agint.[51] Are there other uses of the Hebrew term in the same period that can shed light on early use of the term?

My argument here is that the use of *anawim* in the *The Rule of the Community* from the Dead Sea Scrolls shows a broad understanding of the term more in line with Greek usage. If a single Jewish community understood the Hebrew term *anawim* in a wider sense than the poor or the humble, then the Septuagint translators of Psalm 36:11 may have done so too. Thus a broader reading of Matthew's use of the Greek term would be more plausible.

The Dead Sea Scrolls refer to many manuscripts found in the ruins or caves of the wadis of the Judean desert. Among them are the manuscripts of Qumran written in Hebrew, Aramaic, or Greek found in eleven caves in the area around Khirbet Qumran either through excavation or purchase on the antiquities market. The manuscripts from Qumran are from the period before the destruction of the site in the war against Rome in the first century.[52]

In *The Rule of the Community* (1QS), regulations governing the life of the community may be found. Descriptions of the community, its organization, its self-regulation, and its self-understanding characterize the text. *The Rule of the Community* (hereafter *The Rule*) is a composite text bearing signs of continual revision. It is not possible yet to say whether the existence of several copies in different caves suggests widespread use or an originally single and continuous text. They do suggest shaping of the text over time. *The Rule* opens with a declaration of purpose (although there are lines missing):

> in order to seek God [with all (one's) heart and with all (one's) soul; in order] to do what is good and just in his presence, as commanded by means of the hand of Moses and his servants the Prophets; in order to love everything which he selects and to hate everything that he rejects; in order to keep oneself at a distance from all evil...; to bring about truth, justice and uprightness on earth and not to walk in the stubbornness of a guilty heart and of lecherous eyes performing every evil; in order to welcome into the covenant of kindness all those who freely volunteer to carry out God's decrees....[53]

---

51. LXX Psalms 24:9; 75:10; 147:6; 149:4.
52. Florentino García Martínez, ed. and trans., *The Dead Sea Scrolls Translated: The Qumran Texts in English*, 2d ed. (Leiden: Brill; Grand Rapids, Mich.: Eerdmans, 1996).
53. Ibid., 3.1.

Entering individuals shall establish a covenant before God to carry out commands. In a collective voice they confess sins and are blessed by priests. Curses on outsiders follow, to which the initiands respond "Amen." The priests enter the rule first, followed by the Levites and then all the people "so that all the children of Israel may know their standing in God's Community.... "[54] A statement about the stability of the hierarchy is followed by the rationale: "For all shall be a single Community of truth, of proper meekness, of compassionate love and upright purpose, towards each other in the holy council, associates of an everlasting society." Here the noun "meekness" describes the community of truth. Behind it lies the Hebrew word *anawah*. It is part of a list defining social behavior in the community.

Shortly afterward, in typically dualist language, the document describes the God of Israel and the angel of his truth assisting all the Sons of Light. This is a frequent term describing members of the community. It sets them over and against the Sons of Darkness outside the company. The paths of the Sons of Light in the world are several: to enlighten the heart of man and

> to establish in his heart respect for the precepts of God; it is a spirit of meekness, of patience, generous compassion, eternal goodness, intelligence, understanding, potent wisdom which trusts in all the deeds of God and depends on his abundant mercy; a spirit of knowledge in all the plans of action, of enthusiasm for the decrees of justice, of holy plans with firm purpose, of generous compassion with all the sons of truth, of magnificent purity which detests all unclean idols, of unpretentious behavior with moderation in everything, of prudence in respect of the truth concerning the mysteries of knowledge.[55]

This list of virtues is a description of the inner orientation of a member of the community shaping social behavior. It starts, probably in order of primacy, with the spirit of meekness.

The next passage in *The Rule* concerns the reproof of a community member. "Each should reproach his fellow in truth, in meekness and in compassionate love. No one should speak to his brother in anger or muttering, or with a hard neck or with passionate spiteful intent and he should not detest him in the stubbornness

---

54. 1QS2,18.
55. 1QS3,24–4,6. Cited in García Martínez, *Dead Sea Scrolls*, 6.

of his heart, but instead reproach him that day so as not to incur a sin for his fault."[56] This passage is particularly interesting in that it contrasts anger with meekness and links the latter to compassionate love. The contrast of anger with meekness is also found in Greek texts from Aristotle to Plutarch and the New Testament.

The final passage is fragmentary, but it is part of a section toward the end of the text in which an individual utters a blessing to God. Presumably the individual speaks in the spirit of meekness described in column 4:

> [I shall share out] the regulation with the cord of the ages
> ... justice and compassionate love with the oppressed, and to
> strengthen the hands of the ... understanding of those with
> a stray spirit in order to instruct in the teaching those who
> complain to reply with meekness to the haughty of spirit, and
> with a repentant spirit to the men of the stick, those who
> point the finger and speak evil, and are keen on riches.[57]

In this passage, the purpose clause "in order" is followed by an infinitive, "to instruct." The object of the instruction are those who complain but are taught further to reply with meekness to the haughty. Meekness is thus learned rather than innate. This would accord with the spirit of meekness the individual acquires (col. 1). As we have seen, acquiring meekness is also an idea found in Greek texts.

The interpretation of Psalm 37 in another Dead Sea Scroll text, 4Q171, understands the poor of 37:11 to describe the congregation of the poor.[58]

Thus, four texts from *The Rule* imply that meekness is a dispositional virtue to be learned, that it is the chief characteristic of community members and the whole company, and that it is to be used in a disciplined fashion to reproach a brother. It is also thought of in contrast to anger and haughtiness. All these imply a broader understanding of the Hebrew word *anawah* and the noun "meek" in the first century than one in which it could be seen simply as being humble, poor, or kind. Before we return to Matthew, we must take into account that language describing human

---

56. 1QS5,24–6,1. Cited in ibid., 9.
57. 1QS10,26–11,2. Cited in ibid., 17.
58. 4Q171 cited in ibid., 203–6. 1Q15, the Zephaniah Pesher, is too fragmentary to deduce what might have been made of a "meek and humble people" in 3:12.

qualities or virtues takes place within a context of apocalyptic eschatology.

Apocalyptic Eschatology

Apocalyptic eschatology casts a spell over Matthew's Gospel. It is an all-embracing religious perspective that considers the past, present, and future within a dualistic and deterministic framework.[59] Like the Dead Sea Scrolls, Matthew describes the supernatural world in terms of a cosmic struggle between God and God's agents on the one hand and Satan and the forces of evil on the other. Dualism pervades the cosmos. The world is comprised of good and evil. God's sun shines and the rain falls indiscriminately on the just and the unjust, on the evil and the good.[60] The good and the bad attend weddings,[61] and in the parable of the wheat and the tares, just like that of the dragnet, the good and the rotten fish[62] lead a generally undisturbed life until harvest time or the close of the age when they are sorted. God treats both sets of people apparently without distinction. It is a rationale given for praying for one's enemies and for greeting people other than one's brothers and sisters.[63]

Thus the world is full of undifferentiated good and bad (see table 1). But it is not that simple. Although Jesus himself holds to and teaches absolute distinctions — the good person brings good things out of a good treasure, and the evil person brings evil things out of an evil treasure[64] — he recognizes a disconcerting problem: people can say good things but be evil;[65] they can look righteous but inside be lawless.[66] He himself eschews anger against a brother (5:22) but excoriates the Pharisees (Matt. 23). This is on the one hand a question of perception and on the other a flaw in the moral order, for it means that absolute distinctions do not hold. One solution in Matthew is fragmentation: body parts may be good and healthy or unhealthy and evil. In these cases, one observes which part and what consequences: "The eye is the lamp of the body. If

59. David C. Sim, *Apocalyptic Eschatology in the Gospel of Matthew* (Cambridge: Cambridge University Press, 1996).
60. Matthew 5:45.
61. Matthew 22:10.
62. Matthew 13:48.
63. Matthew 5:44–46.
64. Matthew 12:35.
65. Matthew 12:34.
66. Matthew 23:28.

Table 1

Exhortation/Observation	Virtue	Symptom
"If you, then, who are **evil** know how to give **good** gifts to your children, how much more…" (7:11 NRSV)	**good** and evil (22:10)	How can you speak **good** things, being **evil**? (12:34)
"Friend, **I did not wrong** you" (20:13) "Beware of practicing your **piety** before others" (6:1 NRSV)	**righteous/unrighteous** (5:45)	look **righteous** but inside are lawless (23:28)
does not wish to make an example of a woman (1:19)	**a just man** (1:19)	neglect of **justice, mercy,** and **faith** (23:23)
"I desire mercy, not sacrifice" (9:13 NRSV)		condemns guiltless (12:7)
He will not dispute (12:19)	**"for I am meek and lowly of heart"** (11:29)	exercises authority over (20:25)
"Unless you change and become like children…whoever **humbles** himself like this child" (18:3–4)	your king is coming, **meek** (21:5)	
"you are of more value than birds of the air" (6:26; 10:31)		"fear him who can destroy both soul and body in hell" (10:28; soul and body are of sufficient value to be preserved)
	the sons are **free** (17:26)	boys' lives are expendable (2:16)
"But I say to you, everyone who is **angry** with his brother shall be liable to judgment" (5:22)	a king delays **anger** (18:34)	a king becomes very **angry** in retaliation (2:16)

your eye is healthy, your whole body is full of light, but if your eye is unhealthy, your whole body will be full of darkness. If the light in you is darkness, how great the darkness!"[67] This is an exclama-

---

67. Matthew 6:22–23.

tory observation and nothing more. It addresses the disciples, and
through them the crowds. Elsewhere Jesus recommends the exci-
sion of a body part when it becomes an occasion for stumbling
(18:8–9). Perhaps what is meant is any vice within an individual
leading to sin.

Another solution appears in a context of apocalyptic eschatology. Jesus uses parables to teach that differentiation between good
and bad is to be withheld until the day of judgment when the
angels will divide one from the other. This at least temporarily contains the problem of the duplicity of those who say good things but
who are evil.[68] It defers the conundra of the wheat and the tares
and the good and rotten fish. We can see the puzzle behind the
disciples' question: "Master, did you not sow good seed in your
field? Where, then, did these weeds come from?" (13:27 NRSV).
Since these last two cases appear in parables about the kingdom, it
would not be difficult to argue that Matthew's community is com-
posed of good and bad. The parable solves the problem of their
existence. They are to be left alone until the end. What about right
and wrong?

Behind the English words just/ice and right/eousness (Greek *dikē*
and *dikaiosunē*) or the verbs "to justify" and "to make right" in
Matthew's Gospel (Greek *dikaioō*) lies a single Greek root. The
"many prophets and righteous people" of 13:17 gives the general
meaning of the noun designating a class of the pious in ancient
Israel like the prophets. In Matthew, the righteous are contrasted
with "the unjust" in 5:45 and in 13:49 with "evil ones." Both
Joseph (1:19) and Jesus (27:19) are called "righteous" (*dikaios*) in
Matthew. The narrator describes Joseph as a just man, and Pilate's
wife warns him about Jesus: "Have nothing to do with that righteous man for I have suffered much over him today in a dream."[69]
Jesus himself speaks of the righteous (or innocent) Abel in 23:35.

A group of righteous people is vindicated in the great judgment
for their conduct toward the hungry, or thirsty, or those in prison.
In the judgment scene, the righteous are divided from "those on
the left." Thus righteousness is linked to righteous acts not done
ostentatiously.[70] But they must be done. Jesus himself is baptized

---

68. Matthew 12:36–37.
69. Matthew 27:19. The NRSV translates "innocent man."
70. Matthew 6:1: "Beware of practicing your piety [literally, righteousness] before men in order to be seen by them; for then you will have no reward from your
Father who is in heaven."

by John "to fulfill all righteousness."[71] He warns listeners of the Sermon on the Mount that they will not enter the kingdom "unless their righteousness exceeds that of the scribes and Pharisees."[72] At the end of the sermon, the person who hears his words and does them is compared with a sensible man who built a house on stable foundations. A foolish person hears the words and does nothing.

As a consequence of actions the righteous may expect mistreatment. This Jesus himself mentions with the example of Abel and prophetic figures (23:35). Vindication in the form of eternal life is a future promise while "those on the left" may expect only eternal punishment.[73]

Not only actions but also words cause a person to be justified or condemned on the day of judgment.[74] What about actions or words during one's lifetime? Here the parable of the laborers in the vineyard is helpful. To the laborers hired after the beginning of the day, the owner of the vineyard says: "You also go into the vineyard, and whatever is just, I will pay you."[75] Those hired first, reckoning that they would be paid more at the end of the day, grumbled against the vineyard owner. "Those last ones worked only one hour, and you made them equal to us, the ones who bore the brunt of the day and the heat." The vineyard owner replies to one of them, "Friend, I did not treat you unjustly. Did you not agree with me for a day's wage? Take what is yours and go. For I wish to give to the last what I gave to you. Is it not lawful for me to do what I want with what is mine? Or is your eye evil because I am good?"[76]

The vineyard owner holds to the principle of "what is just" (or right) and chides one who, on another principle (equal work for equal pay), argues against equivalent payment. The vineyard owner is accountable even as he dismisses the grumbler whose eye is evil. The world of moral alternatives (good/evil; what is right or just/what is wrong or unjust) is not bridged, but perception of wrongdoing on the part of the hired laborer causes the vineyard owner to explain the action. His accountability is an important defense of justice in the light of other parables in which no obvious explanation is given for the conduct of the chief subject.

---

71. Matthew 3:15.
72. Matthew 5:20.
73. Matthew 25:46.
74. Matthew 12:37.
75. Matthew 20:4. The NRSV translates "whatever is right."
76. Matthew 20:13–15.

For example, in the parable of the king who gave a wedding banquet for his son, after the invitations have been turned down by the invited guests, the enraged king destroys the murderers of his servants and burns their city. His servants go out and invite whoever they can find, good and bad alike, to the wedding feast. The king notices one of the guests without a wedding garment. When called to account he is silent. The king commands that he be bound hand and foot and cast into outer darkness.[77]

What makes material from *The Rule* so helpful is that, unlike material from Isocrates and Plutarch, both Matthew and the Dead Sea Scrolls share a similar apocalyptic landscape of moral dualism. One cannot appropriate a Greek discussion of any term and conclude that this is Matthew's meaning.[78] As a consequence of Matthew's apocalyptic eschatology, a community consists of good and bad, right and wrong. Individuals are accountable for what they do and say. Sometimes the standards to which they are held accountable are clear, and sometimes they are not. However, all actions are the basis of judgment. Now we can bring this perspective to bear on the notion of the *praus* king.

The *praus* King

The external warrant for interpreting Jesus as king in Matthew 11:28–30 comes from three distinct sources: 21:5, where the adjective *praus* from a Greek translation of Zechariah describes a king; a version of the same passage in the *Gospel of Thomas;* and an interpretation of Matthew 21:5 in the Sibylline Oracles.

The *Gospel of Thomas* preserves what some scholars see as an independent version of Matthew 11:28–30: "Come unto me: for my yoke is easy and my lordship is meek, and you will find repose for yourselves."[79] The case for the independence of the *Gospel of Thomas* from the synoptic Gospels (Matthew, Mark, and Luke) is one to which I subscribe particularly in the case of saying 90. Some of the sayings in the *Gospel of Thomas* are not simply independent of but prior to their counterparts in the synoptic Gospels. For example, the well-known parable of the sower found in Mat-

---

77. Matthew 22:1–14.

78. Perhaps this is the force of Luz's objection. This approach, as we have seen, is taken by commentators on the text from the eighteenth century to the present, including Farrer and Du Bose. It extends to William Barclay, *The Gospel of Matthew,* 2 vols. (Louisville: Westminster/John Knox, 1975), 1:64–66.

79. *Gospel of Thomas* 90, cited in the introduction, p. 7 above.

thew (13:3–9), Mark (4:2–9), and Luke (8:4–8) is also found in
the *Gospel of Thomas* (saying 9),where it is devoid of the allegorical details adorning the versions in the synoptic Gospels. These
allegorical details may reflect the attempts of the Synoptic authors
to adapt aspects of the parable to their own communities and interests. It cannot be accidental that good cases can be made that
the variances in the allegorical details of the synoptic Gospels are
best explained by correspondences in the respective Gospels. Since
the *Gospel of Thomas* has an unadorned version of the parable of
the sower, as it were, it may well be prior to other versions.

Since the *Gospel of Thomas* consists of 114 sayings of Jesus, it
may well correspond to a layer of sayings material in the synoptic Gospels called Q (from the German word *Quelle* [source]). The
closest parallels to the genre represented by the *Gospel of Thomas*
are the Jewish Wisdom books: Proverbs, Wisdom of Sirach, Wisdom of Solomon, and Ecclesiastes.[80] Scholars have attempted to
isolate Q and have posited its existence as a separate source in
the composition of the synoptic Gospels. In the case of Matthew
11:25–30, we have a parallel in Luke (10:21–22) only for verses
25–27. Thus Matthew 11:25–27, like Luke 10:21–22, may derive
from Q, to which Matthew added verses 28–30. As I am arguing in the case of *praus*, there are details in these latter verses best
explained as interests of the Matthean community. The *Gospel of
Thomas* 90 corroborates the independent existence of Matthew
11:28–30, since neither it nor the surrounding material has any
connection to Matthew 11:25–27.

Saying 90 in the *Gospel of Thomas* is an independent version
of Matthew 11:28–30. In the first place, it is much shorter. Saying
90 is primarily about the identity of the speaker: "my yoke is easy
and my lordship is gentle." It does offer the listeners rest. Matthew
11:28–30 identifies those who are addressed ("all who labor and
are heavy-laden") in addition to promising them rest twice. It too
identifies the speaker: a person who speaks with authority using
imperatives ("Come ... take ... learn") and then gives the rationale:
"because I am *praus* and lowly of heart," and again, "for my yoke
is easy and my burden is light."

The aspects Matthew and the *Gospel of Thomas* have in common are the invitation, the rationale, and the promise of rest.

---

80. Helmut Koester, "Introduction to the Gospel According to Thomas," in *Nag
Hammadi Codex II,2–7, Vol. 1,* Nag Hammadi Studies 20, ed. Bentley Layton
(Leiden: Brill, 1989), 44.

Matthew's rationale is longer: "because I am *praus* and lowly of heart," "for my yoke is easy and my burden is light." The *Gospel of Thomas* juxtaposes these two clauses into a single rationale: "for my yoke is easy and my lordship is gentle." I believe that behind the word translated "gentle" (Coptic *rmrash*) lies the Greek word *praus*, although we encounter it here through the Coptic text of the *Gospel of Thomas*. In the Sahidic Coptic translation of the New Testament, *rmrash* translates *praus* at Matthew 11:29, Numbers 12:3, and Zechariah 9:9, where it may be translating the Hebrew or the Greek translation of the Hebrew.[81] Another version of this saying is found in a fourth-century Gnostic text called *Pistis Sophia* 95:

> Because of this now I said to you once: Everyone who is oppressed with care and troubled by their burden, come to me and I will give you rest. For my burden is light and my yoke is *rmrash*.[82]

This is a parallel to Matthew 11:28 and 30 without mention of verse 29. *Pistis Sophia* 140 identifies the yoke as "my lordship," and this connects it with the version found in the *Gospel of Thomas*. Perhaps, however, all three sources are independent of each other.

The Sibylline Oracles cite Matthew's version of Zechariah 9:9 and expound the text by juxtaposing it with Matthew 11:28–30:

> Rejoice, holy daughter Zion, having suffered many things; Your king himself comes in mounted on a foal, appearing meek to all so that he may lift our yoke of slavery, hard to bear, which lies on our neck.[83]

The last warrant for seeing Jesus as king in the passage comes from the immediate context in Matthew 11. The chapter considers questions of identity: John asks his disciples to ask Jesus, "Are you the one who is to come, or should we wait for another?" Jesus "answers" by describing what he does. Jesus asks the crowd what they think of John, whom he subsequently describes as Elijah who is to

---

81. David is described as a *rmrash* king in the *Encomium of Theodosius, Archbishop of Alexandria, on Saint Michael the Archangel*, in *Miscellaneous Coptic Texts in the Dialect of Upper Egypt*, ed. and trans. E. A. Wallis Budge (reprint ed.; New York: AMS Press; 1977), 911.

82. Carl Schmidt, ed., *Pistis Sophia*, Nag Hammadi Studies 9, trans. Violet MacDermot (Leiden: Brill, 1978), 439–40. I have followed the more literal translation.

83. Sibylline Oracles 8.324–28.

come. The present generation describe John as having a demon and Jesus as a glutton, a drunkard, and a friend of tax collectors and sinners. Even these titles vindicate the deeds of wisdom. Ideas about the monarchy thread themselves through the passage. Jesus speaks to the crowds about John the Baptist (v. 7). He chides them for their expectations about him and asks: "Why did you go into the wilderness? To see a reed shaken by the wind?" or "a man adorned luxuriously?" On the contrary, Jesus says, "Those in glorious apparel are in kings' courts." This is followed by a discussion of John's status in the kingdom of heaven. Then comes an enigmatic statement about the violent taking the kingdom of heaven by force (11:12),[84] a criticism of "this generation," and a further criticism of the cities of Chorazin, Capernaum, and Bethsaida: "If the deeds of power which were done in you had been done in Tyre and Sidon, they would have repented. Or if they were done in Sodom, it would have remained until this day."

Most scholars recognize that there is an unexpected change between verse 24 and verse 25.[85] But as we have seen, verses 25–30, like the preceding material, are very much concerned with questions of identity. Moreover, the self-declaration of Jesus, "I am *praus* and lowly of heart" as the disclosure of his identity, is at the same time an answer to the "mighty deeds" of his done in cities and the angry condemnation of verses 20–24 at the rejection of his acts. Instead of anger in retaliation Jesus offers rest, a disclosure of his nature, an easy yoke, and a light burden. These are the words of a *praus* king choosing, in concert with the dualism of the Gospel, not anger but charity. The beatitude of verse 6 works both ways: "Blessed is the one who takes no offense at me" (and if I take no offense at those cities in which mighty works were done).

The demeanor of other kings in the Gospel contrasts with that of Jesus. Jesus' birth takes place in "the days of Herod the king" (2:1). This is the same Herod that we met in the pages of Josephus. Herod's reaction to news of the birth of the child "born king of the Jews" from the mages[86] is fear and terror, and thereafter he reacts

---

84. This is a difficult verse to interpret since the verb *biazetai* can be read as a middle ("the kingdom of God breaks in with power") or a passive ("the kingdom of God is taken violently"). I have taken the latter option as it fits the verse better. Matthew envisages conflict between the forces of good and evil.

85. "Following 11:20–24 one might expect a complaint. Jesus instead offers a prayer of thanksgiving." W. D. Davies and Dale C. Allison, *A Critical and Exegetical Commentary on the Gospel According to Saint Matthew*, 3 vols. (Edinburgh: T. & T. Clark, 1988–97), 2:273.

86. Greek *magoi*. I translate "mages" rather than the usual "wise men."

deviously (see chap. 1). He calls some of his court together: the chief priests and scribes of the people. Through a dream, the mages are warned not to return to Herod after they have found the object of their journey. Learning of this, Herod became extremely angry (2:19) and in reaction kills all the male children born at about the same time as the child of whom the mages spoke.

Two other kings are the subjects of parables. The first, wishing to settle accounts with his servants, is compassionate to a servant who cannot repay debts. Learning that this same servant showed no mercy to a fellow servant similarly indebted to him but had the servant imprisoned, the king has the first servant brought to him. He addresses him: "Wicked servant! All that debt I forgave you since you implored me. Is it not necessary for you also to have mercy on your fellow servant as I had mercy on you?" The text continues, "Having become angry, his lord delivered him to the jailers until he should pay all that he owed" (18:32–34).

In the second parable, a king wishes to give a marriage feast for his son. When the invited guests make their excuses, even maltreating and killing the king's servants, the king becomes angry. He sends his troops, destroys the murderers, and burns their city. He sends his servants to invite anyone they can find on the streets, good and bad alike. Gazing at the assembly and noticing one present who had no wedding garment, the king demands an explanation. Hearing none, he commands the man to be bound hand and foot and cast into outer darkness.

In both these cases, no adjective describes either king. However, both have in common deferred anger, apparently justifiable. In the first example, anger does not emerge until the mistreatment of the one servant by the servant to whom the king showed mercy. The second case is one in which anger is a justifiable response to the unwarranted murder of the king's servants. Both these responses are in contrast to the disproportionate rage of Herod we noted earlier.

That anger, whether justified or not, should occur in all three accounts of kings indicates that anger and sovereignty are linked for Matthew. Anger does not occur elsewhere in regard to any other character in the Gospel.[87] Nor does it occur in regard to Jesus, either when entering Jerusalem as king or at points in the narrative where such an emotional coloring might make sense. For exam-

---

87. The NRSV translates 20:24 and 21:15 in such a way that the ten and the chief priests and scribes "become angry." The RSV translates both passages better: "became indignant. The word in both cases is not the same as the Greek verb at 22:7 and 18:34. The verb at 2:16 is different.

ple, 21:12–17, the cleansing of the temple, is remarkably devoid of emotion. In fact, Matthew alone records that after the cleansing, the blind and the lame came to Jesus in the temple, and he healed them. The reaction of the chief priests and scribes to this is the only emotion in the passage: they become indignant.

To conclude the discussion of anger and sovereignty, some anger on the part of rulers is justifiable. This is particularly the case if the king figures of the parables have anything to do with God. All parables describe a facet of God's reign. In the parables of Matthew's Gospel anger plays a part. However, the violence of Herod's response is unwarranted. Jesus, when seen as a king, is not angry but *praus*. At 11:25–30 he eschews anger. At 21:14–15 he cures the lame and the blind in the temple shortly after he has driven out the moneychangers and has been described as a *praus* king in the text.

Meekness and kingship in the Hellenistic world indicate the self-discipline of an educated ruler who shows compassion for his subjects. This is a consistent pattern of behavior. Matthew's choice of Zechariah 9:9 reflects his interest in this topic, as does his linking of kingship with anger.

As a *praus* king, Jesus enters Jerusalem. At 5:22, he eschews anger since it leads to murder and advocates instead reconciliation as the proper attitude to one's brother. Only God expresses righteous indignation. Just as a Hellenistic king from a position of influence does not advance his own household and friends, neither does Jesus. To the mother of the sons of Zebedee, he says, "To sit at my right hand and my left is not mine to grant, but it is for those for whom it has been prepared by my Father" (20:23). The mode of ruling that should characterize the Matthean community is servanthood, in contrast to the rulers of the Gentiles, whose great ones rule or lord it over them (20:25). One should note that while members of the community are servants to one another, Jesus elsewhere describes their status: "the sons are free" in this case from tax or tribute to earthly kings (17:25–26). For Matthew, Jesus shows what such servanthood is in his free but costly acceptance of God's will, his humble manner, and his subordinate status to God as Son.

What is the demeanor of a *praus* king? To show compassion for others Jesus reassures listeners that they are of great value (6:26; 10:31; 12:12), and he himself shows compassion for others consistently, whatever their response (9:36; 23:37). He tells them to expect no compensation (10:8), and he promises his presence whenever two or three are gathered (18:20). What he teaches to the disciples during their life together is "what has been hidden from the foundation of the world" (13:34–35). In the Great Commission at the end of the Gospel, he reminds the disciples of his earlier teaching as he sends them out to teach (28:20). What one learns is based on the revelation of all things transmitted within the particular relationship of son to father (11:27). If literature from the second temple period knows that "many are lofty and renowned, but to the *praeis* [God] reveals his secrets,"[88] it is also true that meekness in particular individuals is an indication of religious humility: the meekness of Moses in the Greek translation of Numbers 12:3 reflects the unique character of Moses' relationship to God.[89]

The extent of Jesus' meekness may be seen in the refusal to meet aggression with aggression; in response to the hostility of some Pharisees, he withdraws (12:14–21).[90] The addition of the words "he will not wrangle" (12:19) to the citation from Isaiah in Matthew 12:18–21 is a further interpretation of the theme.

What does Jesus teach that exemplifies meekness? First, as we have seen in the antitheses, he teaches the disciples, and through them the community, to avoid anger. Slandering a sibling of the community renders one liable to judgment. Next, he advocates reconciliation rather than lasting enmity between community brethren as the precondition to offering a gift at the altar (5:23–24). In the teaching "do not resist an evil person" (5:39), we have an anticipation of the phrase "he will not wrangle" (12:19), here interpreted for the community. What does the principle of nonretaliation mean?

Retaliation today means to exact revenge. In the realm of ethics it means to "return evil with evil." But the issue of nonretaliation is subordinate to the issue of combating evil. Since evil results in lawlessness (7:23), the combating of evil is undertaken to establish justice. Revenge does not further the cause of justice, for it breaks the law (5:19) and furthers injustice. Nonretaliation defeats evil and furthers the cause of justice.

Further, nonretaliation does not mean a passive acceptance of evil. It is itself a move toward the overcoming of evil. In each

---

88. Sirach 3:20.

89. Dale C. Allison, *The New Moses: A Matthean Typology* (Minneapolis: Fortress, 1993), 218–33.

90. Deirdre J. Good, "The Verb ANACHŌREŌ, to Withdraw, in Matthew's Gospel," *Novum Testamentum* 32/1 (1990): 1–12.

of these cases, the cycle of violence is broken. Turning the other cheek or walking another mile is an active move of a different non-retaliatory nature implying another course of action. It overloads the aggression onto the aggressor by taking the means to extend the aggressive act while at the same time it takes the initiative away from the evil perpetrator. Each of the examples that follow describes an act of violence: being hit, being sued, being forced to accompany someone, and being appealed to for money. The responsive behavior is quite different from what might be expected: turning the other cheek, giving your cloak to one who sues you and takes your coat, going the second mile, and giving to everyone who begs or who wants to borrow from you. All the examples are in the second person singular. This indicates that their exhortatory force is in the direct address to the community member.

Within the Gospel, Jesus himself exemplifies self-conscious and deliberate nonretaliation. When the crowd of mourners "laughs at him" for maintaining that the daughter of the leader of the synagogue is not dead but sleeping, the narrative continues, "Going in, he grasped her hand and raised the young girl" (9:24–25). The mocking crowd is put outside. In response to the beheading of John the Baptist, he withdraws (14:13). To the plotting of some Pharisees intending to snare him in what he said, he chooses not between the alternatives of paying some or no taxes to the emperor but paying to the emperor what is due him and likewise what is due to God (22:15–22).[91] At his arrest, Jesus tells the disciple who takes his sword and cuts off the ear of the high priest's servant: "Put your sword back into its place; for all who take the sword will perish by the sword" (26:52). He specifically says that he will not appeal to the Father to summon legions of angels, and he cites the example of his teaching daily in the temple as a response to a desire to arrest him (26:53–56).

The final teaching about meekness and humility comes in the teaching for the community about the kingdom: "Whoever humbles himself like this child is the greatest in the kingdom of heaven" (18:4). Here the verb with a reflexive pronoun, "to humble oneself," unfortunately lost in the NRSV translation "whoever becomes humble," is important because as an active verb, it in-

---

91. The verb "to snare" (NRSV, "entrap") is unique to Matthew. Behind it lies a deadly aggression. In the LXX, the verb is frequently used to mean "death trap" (e.g., Ps 18:5 [LXX 17:6]): "The cords of Sheol surrounded me, the **snares** of death confronted me." Cf. Jeremiah 18:22; Sirach 9:13; Job 22:10, where the same word in the Greek text describes threats to the righteous.

dicates action that can be done by the individual. Prefacing this teaching is the possibility of change (18:3). Both changing (the Greek means turning) and becoming humble imply volition on the individual's part.

Matthew's use of the motif of Jesus' meekness and humility as conscious nonretaliation resonates within the Gospel and in other contexts. We have already noted that Plutarch advocates a linking of courage and gentleness rather than courage and justice in certain cases of wrongdoing.

Worship of the Meek King

Even while the narrative presents Jesus as an example of servant kingship, Jesus is offered obeisance. People kneel before him from birth. Here, I survey examples of the verb *proskuneō* that we first encountered in the discussion of *proskunēsis* made to Alexander the Great (see chap. 3). When people kneel to him, Jesus is treated like a Hellenistic ruler. To be sure, the verb *proskuneō* appears frequently in the Greek translation of the Hebrew Scriptures, where it signifies both worship of the God of Israel and worship of foreign gods. However, given what we have seen of the veneration of Hellenistic kings and the way Herod's court behaved in Matthew 2, I think it highly likely that the Hellenistic use is the more immediate background to Matthew's understanding of the term.[92] Moreover, in the Gospel, slaves kneel to kings (18:26).

At 2:2 the mages declare their intention to worship Jesus, and at 2:11 they do. At 2:8 Herod proposes the same thing, although the reader infers that this is not a genuine desire. At 8:2 a leper kneels before Jesus and requests healing of this Lord (*kurios*). A leader of the synagogue kneels before him at 9:18. At 15:25 the Canaanite woman does the same thing, calling him Lord (*kurios*). Foreigners like the Caananite woman from a Greek or Roman perspective would be more likely to do this strange thing. The centurion in 8:5 simply appeals to him. Given the history of kingship in Israel and the behavior Josephus ascribes to Herod's court, most Jews of the time would not think such behavior strange.

And yet the text is careful to say "Worship the Lord your God, and serve only him."[93] Perhaps that is because in the context of a discussion between Jesus and Satan, the only alternative to worship

---

92. See, however, 4:10.
93. Matthew 4:10.

of God is worship of Satan (4:9). Jesus himself is worshiped three times by disciples; once at 14:33, after Peter walks on water and twice after the resurrection, when Jesus appears to the women and then to the disciples (28:9, 17).

Since the narrative of Matthew's Gospel twice identifies Jesus as "king of the Jews,"[94] we can ask about monarchic traits. The discussion about *proskuneō* indicates that people prostrate themselves before him. This includes a leper, a leader of the synagogue, foreign mages, and a foreign woman. Although born surrounded by wealth, Jesus, unlike Herod, does not have a court. He does, however, have followers identified as brothers, all of whom address God as Father.[95] On at least one occasion, the mother of two of his followers addresses him as one would a king: "kneeling before him, she asked a favor of him."[96] In response Jesus defers to the authority of the Father. Thus, if Jesus is "king of the Jews," it is within the political context of the client kingship of Herod and the theological context of God as Father.

The best place to see how Matthew envisages Jesus as king in relation to God as Father is in 25:31–46. It is hinted at in the description of Jesus as "one under authority" in 8:9. The judgment story opens with the coming of the Son of Man sitting on the throne of his glory with all the nations gathered before him. After separating the sheep and the goats, the narrative continues:

> Then the king will say to those at his right hand, "Come, you that are blessed by my Father, inherit the kingdom prepared for you from the foundation of the world."[97]

Jesus here is a client king in relation to God the Father. The client king offers the benefaction of the kingdom. The heirs on the right inherit the kingdom. The kingdom itself is the kingdom of God, which John and Jesus proclaim in the Gospel through the ministry of healing and preaching.

Conclusion

The portrait of Jesus as a king, *praus* and humble of heart (11:29–30), is attested in Matthew, the *Gospel of Thomas,* the Sibylline

---

94. Matthew 2:2; 27:37.

95. Here I am thinking of the *adelphoi* in Matthew functioning like the *philoi* of the Hellenistic court. The composition of Matthew's community is a topic for further exploration.

96. Matthew 20:20.

97. Matthew 25:34.

Oracles, and *Pistis Sophia*. It can be shown that this implies rejection of anger, withdrawal from hostility, and refusal to meet
aggression with aggression. Far from being evidence of passive ser-
vility, Jesus' own words to the servant and the crowd at the arrest
and his prayers to God in Gethsemane indicate that humility is
part of choosing obedient sonship to the will of God, even to the
point of death. Jesus' sovereign bearing is seen in contrast to the
demeanor of tyrannical Gentile rulers dominating their subjects
or Herod's anger causing the slaughter of the innocents. This is
Matthew's appropriation of Hellenistic ideas of kingship within a
context of sectarian Judaism.

What implications does this have for human conduct? There are
sensible and foolish people in Matthew whose conduct one can
avoid or emulate. In the case of the righteous or those who say
good things, one can look righteous but be hypocritical and lawless (23:28) or speak good but be evil (12:34).There are those who
neglect justice, mercy, and faith (23:23), and there are wicked servants or unprepared wedding guests who are consigned to prison
or to outer darkness. But from the dichotomy of sensible and foolish, two cognate verbs address a prominent individual and the
Matthean community that indicate a way forward. Jesus tells Peter:
"You are not setting your mind on things of God" (16:23), which
implies that one can set one's mind on things of God and thus
avoid being foolish. And the community is warned: "Take care that
you do not despise one of these little ones" (18:10), suggesting that
community members not disparage or look down on each other.
Since this occurs in the context of "humbling oneself" (18:4), it is
possible that people who did so either were or might be despised.
The Greek verb is a compound verb connected to the same root as
"wise/sensible."

But there is a fundamental difference between Hellenistic authors like Plutarch or Philo and Matthew over the question of
acquisition of *prautēs*. Educated men of the Hellenistic world acquire meekness through discipline and control of emotions. Philo
describes Moses' control of emotions during his adolescence. He
uses philosophical language in which value is attached to control
of the affective aspects of human life through reason. Moses thus
acquires meekness by means of self-discipline. This is also true of
Plutarch's subjects. It is not the case with Jesus. Matthew understands Jesus' meekness to be revealed rather than acquired (11:27).
As part of the revelation of "all things" from the Father, to be
praus and humble of heart is part of his status as dependent and

obedient Son of God. The parameters of filial obedience involve foregoing all exercise of power, as we can see in the rejection of each of the satanic temptations: to make stones bread, to jump off the temple and be rescued by angels, and to possess all the kingdoms of the world (4:3–10). Although the notion of obedient Son is not foreign to other Gospels, it is Matthew alone who articulates the aspect of sonship as revealed and dependent humility and who identifies it as such within the character of Jesus himself. Hence one could say that in respect to the quiet virtues, for Matthew Jesus' gender identity is not acquired but revealed. However, Jesus' teaching of nonretaliation and avoidance of anger ensures that acting out meekness does not wait for revelation. It is also evident when the community speaks liturgically in the corporate voice of dependent child: in the Lord's Prayer to petition the heavenly Father (6:9–13). And prominent individuals among the disciples may themselves receive a revelation of Jesus' sonship (16:15–17).

The admonition in the active verbs "to change" and "to humble oneself" (18:4) is the means whereby Matthew's community appropriates for its members the revelation of Jesus as *praus* and humble of heart. The community is changed by the alteration of each individual. Material from *The Rule of the Community* demonstrates a similar use of meekness as a dispositional virtue enhancing community life within a context of moral dualism. This usage anticipates early Christian use of meekness and humility as communal virtues promoting harmony.

Chapter 5

MEEKNESS IN COMMUNITY

When early Christian groups began to cohere as communities in different parts of the Mediterranean world, various strategies were deployed to create and sustain a common life. We can see one of these in the commendation of the practice of certain quiet virtues in the writings of Paul and James in the New Testament. Later Christians sought to make sense of their origins by tracing a connection from the beginning to their own time. Eusebius, for example, writing in the fourth century, speaks of the first-century Jewish community identified by Philo in Egypt near Lake Mariotis as the Therapeutae and the Therapeutridae as if they were antecedents of Christian communities in his day. In his *Ecclesiastical History*, referring first to apostolic foundations of the church of Alexandria by Mark, Eusebius points out that Philo's Therapeutae were the first Christian monks. He sees in their renunciation of property, in their chastity of life, in their severe fasting, in their solitary lives, in their devotion to scriptural reading, and in other aspects of their ascetic life the Christian monks. Eusebius was so certain that Philo was describing the life of the first Christian monks that he argues that Philo not only knew the life of the first Christian ascetics but also had himself adopted it.[1]

Since the selection of books to form the canon was not fully determined until 386 or shortly thereafter,[2] documents preserved in the New Testament reflect another fourth-century belief about the shape of life in the first century. When we find writers in the New Testament commending *prautēs* and other virtues enhancing community life to recipients of their letters, we may take them at

---

1. Eusebius *Hist. eccl.* 2.16–17.
2. Athanasius's Easter letter is translated in *New Testament Apocrypha*, 2 vols., ET ed. R. McL. Wilson, W. Schneemelcher (Louisville: Westminster John Knox, 1991–92), 1:187.

face value as long as we remember that they reflect a combination of both the ideal and the real.

In this chapter I will explore first a group of texts from the first century commending the practice of particular virtues to promote and sustain community life. There is no particular rationale for the recommendation of these qualities. Some Christian examples of these texts understand certain qualities to reflect the experience of baptism as life in the Spirit as opposed to other qualities that reflect former lives. These texts understand the practice of *prautēs* (or its Hebrew equivalent) to replace a more destructive pattern of behavior, particularly anger. But *prautēs* can be used not simply as a consequence of baptism to combat several situations threatening to destroy a common life. Although writers from the first century of the common era or subsequently do not understand themselves to evoke Aristotle directly, Aristotle's definition of "making *praünsis* as the quieting and appeasing of anger" is a good example of this topic.[3] *Prautēs* promotes community life and friendship. This characteristic commends it to those establishing and wishing to sustain new communities. I will cite examples from Jewish and Christian texts of the common era.

The second group of texts to explore advocate the practice of certain virtues on the basis of their dominical origins. In the Beatitudes, for example, Jesus commends certain types of people. Thus, since what Jesus said became authoritative, especially after the establishment of the canon, later texts commend the *praeis* (the meek) or meek behavior, and those who practice it have the sanction of attempting to follow the words of Jesus.

A third group of texts understands *prautēs* as a power. This fascinating paradox undergirding the practice of *prautēs* or humility in monastic life, for example, deserves exploration.

The Practice of *prautēs*

Texts from the period of Christian origins advocating dispositional virtues for the enhancement of common life presuppose the notion that these virtues must be practiced intentionally. The deliberate cultivation of dispositional virtues like humility, kindness, or compassion is a consequence of putting the well-being of the group first.

---

3. Aristotle *Rh.* 1380A.

Several admonitions to practice dispositional virtues enhancing common life draw from the collective experience of baptism itself seen as a movement from death to life. Baptism is the rite of passage in many (but probably not all) early Christian communities from old life to new. Thus imagery and phraseology of "putting on" a new life with its attendant virtues while at the same time shedding or "taking off" the old way of life occurs in most of these examples. Elaborating on the meaning of baptism allows early Christian writers to draw out the practical consequences of new life for pagan converts. Such people are in turn being "born" into the new community by exercising certain virtues.

A good text to illustrate the practical consequences of new life is Colossians 3. The author of this letter juxtaposes imagery from the death and resurrection of Christ with "getting rid" of traits from the old life and clothing new members with virtues. The text addresses a group using the second person plural: "If then you have been raised with Christ, seek the things above where Christ is, seated at the right hand of God" (v. 1). The rationale is a metaphorical death with Christ. Practically speaking, the letter recipients are to put to death whatever is earthly: "fornication, impurity, passion, evil desire, and greed (which is idolatry)" (v. 5). All these things and others like them must be "set aside... seeing that you have stripped off the old self with its practices and have been clothed with the new" (vv. 9–10). The consequences follow immediately: "Therefore, clothe yourselves as elect of God, holy and beloved, with compassion, mercy, kindness, humility, *prautēs*, patience" (v. 12), and above all, love (v. 14). Value is then attached to the practice of forgiving a complaint, of letting the peace of Christ "rule in your hearts," to being thankful (v. 15), "teaching and admonishing one another in all wisdom" (v. 16), and singing songs to God.

In Colossians 3 the contrast between the old way of life and the new is at first glance oppositional: anger, wrath, malice, and slander (3:8) are contrasted with mercy, kindness, humility, *prautēs*. The contrast between *prautēs* and anger is a standard *topos* of the literature about virtues, and chapter 4 explored this contrast in its own right and as part of a character portrait of kings in Matthew's Gospel. However, closer examination of Colossians reveals that being regulated typifies both the old and the new life. Being regulated by human commands and teachings in the old life indeed seems to be wise in promoting "piety, humility, and severe treatment of the body" (2:22–23). However, such actions are "of no value" and effectively "indulge the flesh." Colossians does not spell out how this happens. The fourth-century sayings of the desert fathers (and mothers) regard such activity within the common life as self-indulgent since it centers on the individual rather than on the well-being of the community. Such evidence from Christian tradition reveals that it was not so easy to shed the old way of life.

First Clement 30, perhaps written in the early second century, also uses baptismal language to enjoin certain kinds of conduct: "Let us put on concord in humbleness of spirit and continence... arrogance and boldness belong to those that are accursed by God, *epieikeia*, humility, and *prautēs* are with those who are blessed by God."[4]

Paul often contrasts behavior he calls the fruit of the Spirit with behavior issuing from the works of the flesh. He closes the letter to the Galatians with examples of both kinds of conduct. Works of the flesh are fornication, impurity, licentiousness, idolatry, sorcery, enmities, strife, jealousy, anger, quarrels, dissension, factions, and so on (5:19–21). The fruit of the Spirit, however, is love, joy, peace, patience, kindness, generosity, faithfulness, *prautēs,* and self-control (5:22–23). Paul says that those who belong to Christ Jesus have crucified the flesh with its passions and desires (5:24). Those who live by the Spirit are guided by it. This means that believers are not conceited or competing against one another, nor do they envy one another.

Paul then gives a specific example of the behavior issuing from such qualities: "*Adelphoi,* if someone is detected in a transgression, you who have received the Spirit should restore such a one in a spirit of *prautēs,* taking care that you yourself are not tested" (6:1). Literature of the period contains many cases illustrating this function of *prautēs.* Second Timothy 2:24–25 decrees that "the Lord's servant [Timothy] must not be quarrelsome but *ēpios* [kindly] to all, an apt teacher, correcting opponents with *prautēs.*" In the same way, at the beginning of the second century Ignatius writes to Polycarp: "If you love good disciples, you have no credit; rather, bring the more troublesome into subjection by *praotēs.* 'Not every wound is healed by the same salve.' 'Stop attacks by embrocations.' "[5] Although Ignatius advises firmness in treatment of the troublesome, use of the word *praotēs* together with two

---

4. 1 Clement 30 in *The Apostolic Fathers,* ed. and trans. Kirsopp Lake, 2 vols., Loeb Classical Library (Cambridge, Mass.: Harvard University Press, 1959), 1:60–61.

5. Ign. *Pol.* 2.1 in William R. Schoedel, *Ignatius of Antioch: A Commentary on*

medical maxims makes two points. The first advocates varying treatment. This is echoed in medical sources[6] and is common advice to philosophers, lawyers, and rulers to be flexible.[7] The second advocates soothing paroxysms (an embrocation is a liquid such as oil and water).

The reproof of a community member in *The Rule of the Community* (see chap. 4) proposes the same conduct in more detail: "Each [member] should reproach his fellow in truth, in meekness and in compassionate love for the man.... No one should speak to his brother in anger or muttering, or with a hard neck, or with passionate spiteful intent and he should not detest him in the stubbornness of his heart, but instead reproach him that day so as not to incur a sin for his fault."[8] Ignatius's advice to Polycarp for the treatment of troublesome folk is based on practical and medical wisdom of the day. While neither Galatians, 2 Timothy, nor *The Rule* spell out a rationale for invoking *prautēs* or its equivalent in matters of community discipline, the sayings of the desert fathers (and mothers) are full of stories advocating restraint or abjuration in judgment on the grounds that a premature or unjust judgment might be made. Galatians 6:1 seems to advocate a conduct of *prautēs* on the grounds that one might find oneself in a similar transgression. If this is the case, the point of *prautēs* is that it prevents a community member from concentrating on the fault of another to the exclusion of (the possibility of) one's own.

The sayings tell a story of Abba (Father) Moses to illustrate this point. He was called to a council to judge a brother who had committed a fault. Moses at first refused to go, but after a brother came to tell him that the whole council was waiting for him, he reluctantly agreed to go. Setting off for the meeting, "he took a leaking jug, filled it with water and carried it with him. The others came out to meet him and said to him, 'What is this, Father?' The

---

the *Letters of Ignatius of Antioch*, Hermeneia (Philadelphia: Fortress, 1985), 262. Ignatius uses the form *praotēs*.

6. Galen, "One drug cannot suit all bodies"; *De compositione medicamentorum* 2.1, in *Claudii Galeni Opera Omnia* (Medicorum Graecorum Opera 1–20) (Leipzig: Cnoblochius, 1821–1833). Cited in Schoedel, *Ignatius of Antioch*, 262 n. 4.

7. E.g., Philo *De Jos.* 33: "The pilot is helped to a successful voyage by means which change with the changes of the wind, and does not confine his guidance of the ship to one method. The physician does not use a single method of treatment for all his patients.... And so too the politician must needs be a man of many sides and many forms." Philo is describing Joseph as a politician assuming a coat of varied colors, "for political life is a thing varied and multiple."

8. 1QS5,24–6,1. See chapter 4, p. 76 above.

old man said to them, 'My sins run out behind me and I do not see them, and today I am coming to judge the errors of another.' When they heard that they said no more to the brother but forgave him."[9] In this story there is a move beyond the texts of Galatians and *The Rule*. Both those texts advocate restraint and compassion in reproach of an erring brother. The story of Abba Moses goes further to suggest that identity with the errant brother is the basis of a greater self-awareness. To advocate use of *prautēs* for the correction of an erring community member in Galatians (or its Hebrew equivalent in *The Rule*) may be moving in this direction.

The *topos* of replacing anger with *prautēs* is well-known and widely used. In the previous chapter I argue that it functions in Matthew's Gospel to describe the conduct of kings. In Matthew 11 Jesus eschews anger in favor of *praus* words. For Aristotle, "becoming angry is the opposite of *praunesthai* [becoming meek]."[10] Becoming meek is then the quieting and appeasing of anger. Aristotle's discussion is worth summarizing since it informs the contrast of anger and *prautēs* in first-century texts.[11] There are, he argues, certain circumstances that induce *praotēs*; if people are angry with those who slight them, then they are not angry with those who do not. Toward those who admit they are sorry for a slight, people cease to be angry. For example, in the treatment of slaves, Aristotle says, we are more likely to be lenient toward and feel less anger for those who admit that they are justly punished. This is because to deny what is evident is disrespect, and disrespect is slight and contempt. *Praotēs* is also induced by the sight of humility on the part of others for they seem to recognize that they are inferior. Recognition of inferiority implies fear, and no one who is afraid slights another. Even the behavior of dogs proves this point, says Aristotle, since dogs do not bite those who sit down or engage in submissive behavior. *Praotēs* is induced when people think they are being treated seriously and when they feel obligated to others for great service. It is induced toward people who do not insult or mock or slight anyone. It is incurred in response to any virtuous individual. Generally speaking, one can determine the reasons that induce

---

9. Moses 2 [PG 65:281D–284A]. Cited in Douglas Burton Christie, *The Word in the Desert: Scripture and the Quest for Holiness in Early Christian Monasticism* (New York: Oxford University Press, 1983), 278.

10. Aristotle *Rh.* 1380A.

11. Hans-Dieter Betz and John M. Dillon, "*De cohibenda ira* (*Moralia* 452E–464D)," in *Plutarch's Ethical Writings*, ed. Hans-Dieter Betz, 170–97, argue that primitive Christianity "stands within a long tradition which took up various contributions from Jewish religion as well as Hellenistic philosophy" (179).

praotēs by considering the opposite. *Praotēs* is induced by fear and respect.

While there is no direct evidence of Aristotle's influence on Christian and Jewish texts of the first century of the common era, nor an analysis of the passion of anger, there is no doubt that Christian and Jewish authors share with Aristotle an understanding that the quality of *prautēs* promotes community. One can practice this quality consciously as an alternative to anger. A good example of this advice to Christians may be found in the exhortations of the Epistle of James:

> Know, my beloved brothers: let everyone be quick to listen, slow to speak, slow to anger; for the anger of a man does not produce God's righteousness. Therefore, rid yourselves of all sordidness and rank growth of wickedness, and with *prautēs* welcome the implanted word that has the power to save your souls.[12]

Here we meet a simpler version of Aristotle's explanation of the conditions inducing *praotēs* tinged with religious language not specifically Christian and not specifically consequent upon baptism. First, there is the exhortation in the address to the letter recipients as *adelphoi* followed by the third person singular imperative: "Let every person be." Then there is the rationale for avoiding anger to produce a state valued from a religious perspective: "For the anger of a man does not produce God's righteousness." This is not explained, but it is held up as a goal to be achieved. One might infer having read Aristotle that anger is a consequence of being slighted, disrespected, contradicted, or being held in contempt and that none of these things is conducive to harmonious community relations in one early Christian community. The attitude commended by the author of the epistle is to listen and receive the "implanted word." The next sentence commends "doing," not simply "hearing."

There is a lengthy discussion of the avoidance of anger in the early Christian *Shepherd of Hermas Mandates* 5.[13] If one is long-suffering (*makrothumia*), the Holy Spirit has room to dwell within the individual. Anger, however, being associated with the devil,

---

12. James 1:19–21. My translation is more literal than that of the NRSV in keeping to the Greek text and the word order.

13. The rare word "anger" (Greek *oxucholia*) does not occur in Paul or Plutarch. *Mandate* 5 is in "The Shepherd of Hermas," in *The Apostolic Fathers* 2, ed. and trans. Kirsopp Lake, Loeb Classical Library (Cambridge, Mass.: Harvard University Press, 1959).

chokes the Holy Spirit and causes its departure. It works on those who are vain and double-minded. One can escape anger only by being long-suffering since it "is great and mighty and has steadfast power and prospers in great breadth, is joyful, glad, without care, 'glorifying the Lord at every time' has nothing bitter in itself, but remains always *praeia* and *hesuchios.*"[14] Here we see a different approach to the same topic. The Holy Spirit dwells with *praotēs* and *hesychia* and is induced by the behavior described as *makrothumia*. Its application to the individual rather than the common life is stressed.

Gregory of Nyssa (b. 335), one of the great theologians of the eastern Christian tradition, wrote a series of homilies on the Beatitudes.[15] Occupied throughout his life with the question of the vision and knowledge of God, he argues that humans ought to strive to know God as far as possible. He takes it for granted that we can know God through our natural reason, but the vision of God in the mirror of the pure soul can be attained only by Christians. If a human life is pure, the original image in which he was created will shine forth. By contemplating this image in ourselves we can form a conception of the divine perfections. Development of the virtues permits the original beauty of the soul to reappear. Virtues like purity and freedom from passions lead to sanctity and establish the kingdom of God by restoring the image.

In sermon 2 entitled "Blessed are the *praeis,* for they shall inherit the land," Gregory considers the virtue by the same name. Human character is divided into opposite impulses with the natural inclination to be drawn to passion. Those who are blessed are not easily turned toward the passionate movements of the soul but are steadied by reason. The reasoning power acts like a restraint. *Praotēs* acts, for example, in relation to its opposite, anger. When a word or deed arouses this faculty, a person becomes enraged and overcome by the passion of anger. In that state one can still be guided by the beatitude to subduing (*katapraunein*) the malady through reason. One can cultivate a calm expression and a gentle voice.

According to Gregory, that this beatitude has anger in mind is shown by the order of the Beatitudes. Following the one enjoining us to be *tapeinophrosunē,* this one builds on the well-established quality, since if you free a character of pride, the passion of anger

---

14. *Hermas Mandates* 5.2.3.
15. Gregory of Nyssa, *Gregorii Nysseni, de Oratione Dominica; de Beatitudinibus,* ed. Johannes F. Callahan (Leiden and New York: Brill, 1992), 75–170.

has no chance of springing up. Insult or the threat of dishonor does not affect a man trained in humility. "For if he has purged his mind of human deceit, he will look at the lowliness of the nature allotted to him." "If a man sees these things clearly with the purified eye of the soul, he will not easily be annoyed by the absence of honors. The honor of the soul does not consist in things coveted by this world. Riches or fame or self-esteem are destruction and shame to the honor of the soul. If humility is well-established, anger will find no entrance into the soul. And if anger is absent, life will be in a settled state of peace." And this is nothing other than *prautēs,* "the end of which is beatitude and the inheritance of the heavenly country in Christ Jesus to whom be glory and dominion for ever. Amen."[16]

At about the same time, the desert fathers and mothers were wrestling with the problem of anger by proposing various strategies to overcome it. Abba Evagrius called anger "the most fierce passion" and described it in language reminiscent of Gregory of Nyssa: "It constantly irritates the soul and above all at the time of prayer it seizes the mind and flashes a picture of the offensive person before one's eyes."[17] Indignation is followed by a general debility of the body, malnutrition with its attendant pallor, and the illusion of being attacked by poisonous wild beasts. The grip of anger was fierce and tenacious. Abba Ammonas declares himself to have spent fourteen years asking God to grant him the victory over anger.

A concrete expression of this resistance to anger was the refusal to retaliate. However, this had to be accompanied by action. "If someone does you wrong, do good to him," counseled Abba John Colobos. Careful reflection on the discipline needed to protect even facial expressions from reflecting anger led to an understanding of prayer defined by Abba Evagrius as "the seed of gentleness and the absence of malice."[18] Another strategy was to remove oneself physically from a situation in which one might express anger.

---

16. A similar argument is made by a sermon attributed to John Chrysostom, *De mansuetudine sermo* (PL 63:549–55) hitherto untranslated. *Praotēs* leads to *philanthrōpia.* This is not simply the absence of anger and envy but in fact the most important virtue a Christian can practice.

17. Christie, *The Word,* 267.

18. Nilus 2 [PG 65:305B]. Cited in Christie, *The Word,* 270. Christie understands love to be the countervailing force to anger rather than meekness in the sayings of the desert fathers. He does not attach particular importance to this quotation. I am not proposing to replace love with meekness, merely to give this virtue its due weight in the writings from the desert.

The texts from Colossians, 1 Clement, and Galatians include *prautēs* in lists of commendable virtues as part of new life in the Spirit consequent upon baptism. The quality of *prautēs* itself does not derive from a character trait in the life of a famous man known to the letter recipients. It belongs in a list of virtues enhancing community life. Application of *prautēs* has at least two practical consequences: it may be used successfully to discipline members of the community (Gal.; *The Rule*) or opponents (Ign. *Pol.*; 2 Tim.), and that is because *prautēs* may be evoked as an alternative to anger. That this is not a specifically Christian application of certain qualities may be seen by use of the same rationale for correcting community members in *The Rule* from the Dead Sea Scrolls. However, since all these texts date from no later than the first or early second century and each prescribes community regulations, what they have in common is interest in successful intra- (and in the case of Ignatius and 2 Timothy, extra-) group relations.

A reference to Matthew 5:5 may be found in *Didache* 3. *Didache* (or *Teaching*) is usually dated toward the end of the first century, perhaps even as early as 50 c.e., and is linked in particular with Matthew's Gospel.[19] Chapter 3 contains advice to an individual, perhaps a new convert. The individual is advised to eschew pride, lust, an interest in omens, and not to become a magician, an enchanter, an astrologer or a liar. "My child," the text continues, "do not be a grumbler, for this leads to blasphemy, nor stubborn, nor a thinker of evil for from all of these are blasphemies engendered, but be '*praus,* for the *praeis* will inherit the earth.'" The passive aspect of this quality is emphasized by the next paragraph: "Be *makrothumos,* and merciful and guileless and *hesuchios* and good, and fearing the words which you have heard. You will not exalt yourself, nor give your soul to presumption. Your soul will not consort with the lofty, but you will conduct yourself with righteous and humble people. What happens to you, receive as good things, knowing that nothing happens without God."

It may be the case that texts in which *prautēs* is one of several virtues practiced as life in the Spirit consequent on baptism belong to a milieu wherein converts are non-Jewish or pagan (Gentile) in origin. Matthew contrasts anger with *praus* behavior; James eschews anger in favor of welcoming teaching with *prautēs.* Neither describes this or any other commendable virtue as having any-

---

19. Jean-Paul Audet, *La Didachè: Instructions des Apôtres* (Paris: J. Gabalda, 1958).

thing to do with baptism. Both belong in a Jewish milieu. A third text, the *Didache*, enjoins new converts to be *praeis* amongst other qualities as part of its catechetical instruction. Baptism follows the injunction to be *praeis* as it does in the case of Matthew's Gospel.

Humility

The desert fathers and mothers of the fourth century gave much thought to the quality of humility. Abba John of Thebes said: "First of all, the monk must gain humility; for it is the first commandment of the Lord who said: Blessed are the poor in spirit, for theirs is the kingdom of heaven."[20] Humility was the starting point for the desert monks, in part because it was the first beatitude from Jesus and in part because the self-emptying it implied embodied the withdrawal they had come to the desert to find. The monks and nuns sought to live out in their lives the meaning of the words and example of Jesus.

For Abba Poemen humility was the breath of life itself: "As the breath which comes out of his nostrils, so does a man need humility and the fear of God."[21] Amma Syncletica noted that it was humility that held the monk's life together and made salvation possible: "Just as one cannot build a ship unless one has some nails, so it is impossible to be saved without humility."[22] Humility held pride of place in relation to all the other virtues; it was held to be superior to feats of asceticism, vigils, any kind of suffering, or acts demonstrating personal achievement.

Cultivating a sense of humility for the desert fathers and mothers meant fostering both a sense of one's own sinfulness and a sense of one's utter dependence on God's mercy. The possibility of self-deception was ever present. Abba Arsenius considered carefully what it meant to take on the yoke of Christ's humility. He did this after watching several people engaging in futile efforts. One was pouring water from the lake into a broken receptacle so that the water ran back into the lake. Two men on horseback tried to carry a crossbeam of wood through a doorway. Because they refused to dismount the beam would not fit through the door, and neither could they. Then a voice spoke to Arsenius: "These men carry the

---

20. John of Thebes 1 [PG 65:233D]. Cited in Christie, *The Word*, 236.
21. Poemen 49 [PG 65:333B]. Cited in ibid., 237.
22. Syncletica 26. In Jean-Claude Guy, *Recherches sur la tradition grecque des Apophthegmata Patrum*, Subsidia Hagiographica 36. (Brussels: Société des Bollandistes, 1962), S9, 35.

yoke of righteousness with pride, and do not humble themselves so as to correct themselves and walk in the humble way of Christ. So they remain outside the Kingdom of God. . . . Everyone must be watchful of his actions lest he labor in vain."[23]

The people Arsenius observes are reflections of himself working at various tasks. Yet none of their work is effective. Their mistake is that they carry the yoke of righteousness with pride and do not humble themselves. This argument recalls the invitation of Jesus in Matthew 11:29 to "take my yoke upon you for I am *praus* and *tapeinos* of heart," and the injunction of Jesus in Matthew 18:4: "whoever humbles himself like this little child is the greatest in the kingdom of heaven."[24]

The Power of Meekness

In order to discuss this topic, we must remind ourselves of the notion discussed in chapters 3 and 4 that an individual leader demonstrates qualities in demeanor and actions. When this common idea found expression in early Christian writings, it was in connection with discussions of leadership qualities. Moreover, Christians themselves were enjoined to take on these qualities.

One example is found in the letters of Ignatius of Antioch. He writes to several groups of Christians in communities at the western end of Asia Minor in the early part of the second century. A bishop of Antioch, Ignatius was widely regarded as a martyr, and the early date of his writings marks them as an important source for early reflection on theology, the person of Christ, and offices in the churches, including the episcopate.[25]

It is clear that the ill-treatment Ignatius himself has received is part of a wider pattern in which the Christians to whom Ignatius wrote are also mistreated for their faith. In advising them not to

---

23. Arsenius 33 [PG 65:100CD–101A]. Cited in Christie, *The Word*, 242.

24. Greek *tapeinōsei heauton* is the same as the Greek in the vision of Abba Arsenius: *etapeinōthēsan heatous*. Christie thinks the scriptural allusion in the story is to the image of Christ "humbling himself" in the famous hymn of Philippians 2. This is as possible as the allusion to Matthew 18 for which I have argued. Whether Philippians 2 lies behind Arsenius's vision depends on how far the monks would have been prepared to understand their exercise of *imitatio Christi*.

25. Schoedel, *Ignatius of Antioch*. Modern scholarship on the text of Ignatius begins with the work of the Anglican bishop James Ussher in 1644 and continues in J. B. Lightfoot, *The Apostolic Fathers, Part 2: S. Ignatius, S. Polycarp*, 3 vols. (London: Macmillan, 1885), 1:127–221. Ussher brought to light the so-called middle recension of the text of Ignatius (represented by only one manuscript of the eleventh century) and now regarded as the most reliable form of the text.

resist anger, Ignatius draws on several ideas we have discussed: the widespread theme of replacing anger with *praus* behavior; the example of Christ and his words; and the understanding of *epieikeia* between *adelphoi* discussed in chapter 2:

> Before their anger be *praeis;* before their boastfulness be humble; before their slanderings [offer] prayers; before their deceit be fixed in faith; before their fierceness be mild, not being eager to imitate them in return. Let us be found their *adelphoi* in *epieikeia;* let us be eager to be imitators of the Lord — who was wronged more? who was defrauded more? who was rejected more? — so that no plant of the devil may be found among you, but that in all purity and sobriety you may abide in Jesus Christ, in flesh and in spirit.[26]

In this passage we find that the discourse functions in two ways. First there is the public exoteric message in which the reader is encouraged to adopt qualities of subservience in imitation of Christ. Here we might well be reading an echo of Matthew 5:5. This is acceptable behavior on the part of a persecuted subordinate group to dominant outsiders. But behind the discourse is a coded message. Since Jesus the *praus* king (or any other Hellenistic king) is a well-known model for subservient behavior toward the more powerful, the *praeis* by their conduct are subverting those in positions of power just as Jesus did. The powerful persecutors are overthrown by the behavior of the *praeis*. In this way, to be *praeis* is read in code as "to be strong." But this esoteric message is only known to the *praeis* themselves and read as a coded message through the ordinary discourse.[27]

That the intention of the passage is to claim power is evident in the mention of persons of higher status: *adelphoi* and the devil. Ignatius exhorts readers to be found *adelphoi* of the persecutors. Why use this image? First because of the association of *praus* and *epieikeia* with the idea of brotherhood. Siblings have claims of at least equal status on each other. Ignatius then adds a further aim: "that no plant of the devil be found in you." How the practice of qualities like purity and sobriety may be understood to oppose the devil is not self-evident. My point is that even if the discourse is coded and somewhat obscure, the stakes are high. One does not

---

26. Ign. *Eph.* 10.1–3. My translation draws on that of Schoedel, *Ignatius of Antioch*, 69.

27. James C. Scott, *Domination and the Arts of Resistance* (New Haven, Conn., and London: Yale University Press, 1990).

practice these or any other virtues for their own sake but rather because they oppose evil.

A good way to interpret any text, as we know, is to use that text to interpret itself. Light is shed on the coded message of the passage to the Ephesians by the letter to the Trallians. Ignatius speaks first of the need to be subordinate to the Trallian bishop and then of the office. "Do nothing without the bishop," he says, and "be subject also to the presbytery."[28] Everyone ought to respect the deacons as Jesus Christ, and the bishop as a type of the Father, and the presbyters as a council of God and the apostles. Ignatius knows they accept this, for he has received, he tells them, "the exemplar of your love, and I have it with me in your bishop whose very demeanor is a great lesson and his *praotēs* is a great power, whom I think even the atheists respect."[29] Ignatius is saying that subordination is power. This is the code to read behind every injunction to submissive behavior in the Ignatian epistles. As it is exemplified in the person of the bishop, so it may be practiced by the recipients of the letter.

Having praised the Trallians, the language of the next section goes on to criticize them carefully. Like Paul, Ignatius follows Hellenistic models such as Plutarch[30] in qualifying the boasting apparently imposed on him by the situation. He is sensitive to the dangers of self-praise, and he knows that this danger may open the way for the devil. Although he has "much knowledge,"[31] he must "measure" himself, just as Paul will not let his boasting go "beyond measure"[32] and as Plutarch admires Achilles because he ascribed glory to the deity "and was moderate."[33]

However, as William R. Schoedel notes, Ignatius's world is more intense than that of Plutarch. His own situation of persecution and imminent death gives an almost frenzied quality to his writing. He connects a concern about his possible unworthiness with temptations to self-assertion. Feelings of pride are awakened by those who speak to him of his martyrdom. "I love to suffer," he says.[34] However, temptations to assert himself call his commitment into question. These temptations are so strong and so powerful

---

28. Ign. *Trall.* 2.2.
29. Ibid., 3.2–3.
30. Plutarch *De laude ipsius* 539D.
31. Ign. *Trall.* 4.1.
32. 2 Corinthians 10:13.
33. Plutarch *De laude ipsius* 541C. Cited in Schoedel, *Ignatius of Antioch*, 144.
34. Ign. *Trall.* 4.2.

that Ignatius attributes them to the "envy" of supernatural forces. What instills pride in him is satanic. It is possible that this has to do with Ignatius's personality traits. Perhaps he had a tendency to self-aggrandizement. He closes the passage with a striking personal statement: "Since [envy] fights against me the more; therefore I need *praotēs* by which the ruler of this age is destroyed."[35]

The same kind of power in humility may be seen in stories from the later desert fathers and mothers describing most dramatically the monk's (or nun's) capacity to overcome the haunting forces of demonic attacks.[36] Such stories symbolize mastery over the inner world: the monk or nun who had embraced obscurity, humility, and self-negation yet wielded extraordinary strength against powers arrayed against them. How a presence in absence manifested itself was of great interest to the monks and nuns. Daily recitation of Scripture was a way of life and a source of encouragement in the struggles of the desert folk as they fought against the demonic forces. Even more efficacious than this recitation of Scripture, however, and the end toward which all recitation of Scripture was meant to lead, was the realization of Scripture in one's life. The realization of humility was seen to give the monks and nuns unusual power over the evil forces that plagued them.[37]

In one instance, a demon approached Macarius with a knife and tried to cut his foot. However, "because of Macarius' humility, he could not do so. He said to Macarius, 'All that you have, we have also; you are distinguished from us only by humility; by that you get the better of us.' "[38]

Sometimes the stories of the desert show Ignatius in a sharper light. Never does Ignatius wrestle with the contrast and potential conflict between holding an office (whether bishop or presbyter or deacon) and practicing *praotēs*. Among the desert monks and nuns, those who showed themselves uninterested in either seeking or preserving such status provided living examples of the practice of humility. For many of the elders, ordination was something to be avoided at all cost. For one thing, it was felt to be only for those

---

35. Ign. *Trall.* 4.2. Cf. 8.1–2: "Not because I know of any such thing among you, but I want to put you whom I love on your guard, foreseeing the snares of the devil. You then, take up *praupatheia* and renew yourselves in faith — which is the flesh of the Lord — and in love which is the blood of Jesus Christ."

36. Christie, *The Word*, 256–58.

37. Ibid., 256.

38. Macarius the Great 35 [PG 65:277CD]; see also Theodora 6 [PG 65:240B], where the demons claim, "nothing can overcome us, but only humility." Cited in Christie, *The Word*, 256 and note 63.

who were "without reproach," and rarely did the monks see themselves as worthy. Also the status and honor accompanying such offices were felt to be nuisances or even worse, impediments to salvation. During a journey with a companion in the desert near Mount Sinai, Abba Matoes was seized by a local bishop and ordained a priest. Matoes expresses his reservations: "I did not wish it to be sure; but what really troubles me is that I must be separated from the brother who is with me and I am not able to keep on saying the prayers quite alone." The bishop, wishing to accommodate Matoes, asked him whether his brother was ready for ordination. Matoes said, "I do not know if he is worthy of it; I know only one thing, that he is better than I." So the bishop ordained the brother also. But in spite of their ordinations, neither of them even approached the sanctuary to celebrate the Eucharist. Their sense of unworthiness kept them away.[39] Others who had been ordained were similarly reserved about their status and showed real sensitivity for the feelings of others. "Peter, priest of Dios, when he prayed with others, ought to have stood in front, because he was a priest. But because of his humility, he stood behind." Nor did he make a show of this humility. Rather, "he did this without annoying anyone."[40]

Only realization of humility within oneself gives a desert monk or nun the power to dispel evil. "There came certain folk to an old man in the Thebaid, bringing with them one vexed by a devil, that the old man might heal him. After much pleading, the old man said to the devil, 'Go out from this that God made.' And the devil answered, 'I go, but I ask thee one question, and do thou answer me: who be the goats and who the lambs?' And the old man said, 'The goats indeed be such as I; but who the lambs may be, God knows.' And hearing it the devil cried out with a great voice, 'Behold, because of this humbleness of thine, I go.' And he went out that same hour."[41]

Another story has the same theme: "The devil appeared to a certain brother transformed into an angel of light, and said to him, 'I am the angel Gabriel and I am sent unto thee.' But he said, 'Look

39. Matoes 9 [PG 65:292C–293A]. Cited in ibid., 251.
40. Peter of Dios [PG 65:385C]. Cited in ibid., 252.
41. Helen Waddell, *The Desert Fathers* (London: Constable, 1936), 169. Waddell found the sayings to hold her "then, as now, with [their] strange timelessness." She calls her selection "fragmentary and arbitrary," "but it represents that part of the Desert teaching most alien and most sovereign in a world that has fallen to the ancient anarchs of cruelty and pride."

to it that thou wast not sent to some other; for I am not worthy
that an angel should be sent to me.' And the devil was no more
seen."[42]

Perhaps the best example of how this power worked in the life
of the monk is in the story about a demon-possessed girl and the
healing power of some anchorites. The story relates how a monk
who knew the family of the girl told her father: "No one can heal
your daughter except some anchorites whom I know, but if you
ask them to do so, they will not agree because of their humility."
To get around this difficulty he proposed a ruse: "When they come
to the market, you should look as though you want to buy their
goods. When they come to receive the price, we will ask them to
say a prayer and I believe she will be healed." The two men went
to the market, where they found a disciple of the anchorites selling
their goods. They led him away with his baskets, ostensibly to pay
him but in reality to ask him to say a prayer. When they reached
the house, their carefully prepared plan came unraveled, for the
demon-possessed girl ran from the house and slapped the disciple
across the face. But,

> he only turned the other cheek, according to the Lord's com-
> mand [Matt. 5:39]. The devil, tortured by this, cried out,
> "What violence! The commandment of Jesus drives me out."
> Immediately, the woman was cleansed. When the anchorites
> came, they heard what had happened and glorified God say-
> ing, "This is how the pride of the devil is brought low,
> through the humility of the commandment of Christ."[43]

Here we see at work the efficacy of humility as a force in the lives
of the desert monks. We also see the way in which the paradox of
humility as a power brings out the coded message of Jesus' saying, "Turn the other cheek." What looks like self-effacement is in
fact a coded way of describing hidden strength. The anchorites'
unwillingness to heal is not seen as callous neglect but rather as an
example of their holiness. Their humility prevents them from even
considering a public display of power. Prompt action on the part of
the anchorites' disciple stems from the internalization of Scripture.
The demon was driven out by a commandment realized in action.
The statement the demon utters upon departing reminds us what
it meant for the desert fathers and mothers to interpret a biblical

42. Ibid., 169.
43. Christie, *The Word*, 257.

text fully; the meaning of a text could be realized completely only through action. The power to engage in such an action depended on the humility of the actor appropriating the text on a very deep level — in a sense to have become the text.[44]

Conclusion

That the deliberate cultivation of humility, *prautēs*, or other qualities of self-denial potentially enhanced the common life of first-century communities may be more plausibly argued from the fourth-century writings of the desert fathers and mothers and the lives of men and women in the monastic communities of Christian tradition. Appropriating the biblical mandate meant putting it into practice. Acquiring an attitude of dependence follows the mandates of Jesus in the Gospels and exemplifies, in some cases, new life in the Spirit. In the case of Ignatius, injunctions to subservience encode the promise of overcoming those to whom one is subordinate since they are based on the model of a *praus* king refusing to exercise power tyrannically, whether Jesus himself or other Hellenistic rulers. Hellenistic royal ideology is annexed in the service of community virtues. This paradox of power as the absence of power is a legacy of these texts and the reality they reflect, however dimly.

---

44. Ibid., 258.

CONCLUSION

This study has investigated several Greek texts from the first century B.C.E. to the fourth century C.E. in which the word *praus* or a cognate appears in a variety of contexts. Modern translations of these texts identifying individuals or groups as "meek" with the connotation "submissive" or "humble" restrict the meaning of the Greek term. They also allow a pejorative connotation of submitting tamely to oppression or injury to determine the meaning of the word. Readers of ancient Greek and Hebrew texts together with English translations of them until the early part of the twentieth century understood the word and its preferred translation "meek" to convey a wider range of meaning. The present study attempts to convey some of the connotations of the English word "meek" especially as it reflects a range of meaning in its translation of Greek texts.

In Greek antiquity, the word first appears as a quality within a context in which women and slaves are commended for their quiet virtues and men are commended for prowess in competition and public demonstrations of excellence. Later, from the time of Aristotle and Plato onward, the quiet virtues of slaves and women came to replace the competitive ones of male heroes, probably because of their social benefits. Traces of this older association, however, never disappear. They persist in Sirach 36:23 (LXX): "If kindness and *prautēs* mark [a wife's] speech, her husband is more fortunate than other men,"[1] and 1 Peter 3:4: "[Wives], let your adornment be the inner self with the lasting beauty of a *praus* and quiet spirit, which is very precious in God's sight." Similarly, Titus 2:9 exhorts slaves to "be submissive to their masters and to give satisfaction in every respect; they are not to be refractory, nor to pilfer, but to show entire and true fidelity, so that in everything they may adorn the doctrine of God our Savior."

---

1. Cf. Sirach 36:22–23.

While Hellenistic writers like Plutarch understand men to be *praus* by nature, reason, education, and even marriage may persuade women to become *praus*. Both Plutarch and Philo describe in detail the training and self-discipline required of male leaders. In Isocrates and Xenophon, the notion of *praotēs* is present not just ideologically as an expression of a patriarchal society. Nations, humans, and domestic animals like horses also need discipline. In Plutarch's discussion, *De cohibenda ira,* men who lead exercise compassion (*praotēs* induced through rational control), while women, like other less powerful creatures, display only rage. Angry or irrational men import anger from the women's to the men's quarters. Like women without training or education, older men and slaves have no means to educate a latent capacity for compassion toward others. Any of these three groups brought into contact with heads of households or other men in positions of authority can be encouraged to exercise the self-control of compassion toward others. For example, the magic of philosophy weaves a spell over those entering into marriage, by which both women and men become amiable and *praos*. Reason persuades women to set aside luxuries *praōs* (meekly) and thus practice moderation.[2] Plutarch argues that while training leaders can induce *praotēs,* other factors such as gender, social status, and one's own nature promote its appearance.

In a similar manner, Pauline texts and the Pastoral Epistles describe leaders wielding power through compassion rather than coercion (1 Cor. 4:14–21; 2 Cor. 10:1; 2 Tim. 2:24–25). Ignatius of Antioch identifies the bishop's *praotēs* as a great power (Ign. *Trall.* 3.1–4.2). Jesus also demonstrates this quality of his leadership in the *Gospel of Thomas* saying 90.

While the term describes Jesus only twice (Matt. 11:29; 21:5), it is as a *praus* king on the model of Hellenistic kingship that Jesus presents himself in Matthew's Gospel. In contrast to other kings in the text, particularly the Roman client king Herod the Great, who is described as alternately fearful and exceedingly angry (Matt. 2), or the Gentile rulers who "lord it over" their subjects (20:25), Jesus eschews anger in 11:27–30, will not dispute (12:19), and rejects retaliation even at the point of death (26:51–56). Like a Hellenistic male, Jesus consciously exercises virtues, even those acquired through revelation. The whole value structure of Jesus in Matthew's Gospel is in sharpest contrast to that of the Roman

---

2. Plutarch *Coniugalia praecepta* (*Moralia* 138B–146A) 138C; 139E.

client king Herod. While to Herod, boys' lives are expendable (2:16), to Jesus the sons of the kingdom of heaven are free (17:26), and the disciples are of more value than birds of the air (6:26; 10:31). Like his earthly father, Joseph, who does not wish to make an example of a woman (1:19), Jesus understands the voice of God his heavenly Father to "desire mercy and not sacrifice" (9:13). And yet like Herod in the Gospel, Jesus functions as a client king dependent on his Father in heaven. At the judgment scene of 25:31–46 as Son of Man and king, Jesus offers the kingdom of his Father as the inheritance of those on the right hand.

In early communities, whether Christian or Jewish, dispositional qualities enhancing a common life are commended to adherents. In Christian groups these qualities are sometimes thought to reflect the ideal life of the catechumens preparing to enter the communities (*Did.*; Matt.; perhaps James), while in other texts these same qualities reflect postbaptismal new life in the spirit (Col.; Gal.; 1 Clem.). This difference may reflect varying origins of the outsiders.

Several texts from either group (Gal.; Ign. *Pol.*) and Jewish texts (*The Rule*) commend the exercise of compassion rather than anger in the matter of disciplining an erring brother (member of the community) or toward opponents (2 Tim.). James, Plutarch, and the *Shepherd of Hermas* simply condemn anger. Such texts reflect a well-known topic reflected in early Stoic writings (Seneca *De ira*), where it meant freedom from the passion of anger. According to Plutarch (*De coh. ira*), anger is one of the passions and a disease of the soul that must be eradicated. Symptoms may be detected and underlying causes analyzed to be reasoned away, while at the same time one should avoid occasions of provocation. The fourth-century Gregory of Nyssa brings this traditional topic to bear on his sermonic interpretation of the beatitude "Blessed are the *praeis*, for they shall inherit the land" by showing how reasoning power acting as a restraint subdues the malady of anger.

Finally, the fascinating paradox of the power of meekness overcoming diabolic forces, implicit in some early Christian texts, may be seen in Ignatius's letter to the Trallians and some of the fourth-century writings of the desert fathers and mothers. Behind the public message of these texts commending subservience is the hidden message mediated through the triumphant model of Jesus the meek king (Matt.; Phil. 2) that self-abnegation is a form of power. And yet one cannot pursue this form of power except through the constant preparedness for circumstances in which to exercise humility. Only this gives the desert monk or nun the ability to dispel evil.

The range, diversity, and richness of these ancient texts reveal a world of values in which the virtues of leaders and followers intersect. Something of this range informs the English word "meek" and calls for meekness to be liberated from the nativity of Jesus.

EPILOGUE

The word "meek" came into the English language from the Scandinavian in the early Middle English period.[1] Its appearance in Tyndale's translation (1530–34) of Matthew 5:5; 11:29; 21:5 and elsewhere does not appear to derive from Martin Luther's translation of Matthew 5:5, "Sanftmütigen," or 11:29, "ich bin sanftmütig und von Herzen demütig," or 21:5, "dein König kommt zu dir sanftmütig." Tyndale may have read any of the numerous Wycliffite tracts, but it seems unlikely that he used their particular Bible translations. It is worth noting, however, that the Wycliffite translation, which Wycliffe probably inspired, translated Matthew 11:29:

> Take ȝe my ȝoc vpon ȝou, and 'lerne ȝe of me, for I am mylde and meeke in herte; and ȝe shulen fynde reste in ȝoure soulis.[2]

Tyndale explains how he understands his translation of Matthew 5:5: "Blessed are the meke: for they shall inheret the erth." If trouble arise, and we are patient and abide, the end will go on our side. Of course it is impossible to live anywhere without vexation. If it should happen by accident, then forgiveness is reasonable. If the wrong done you is greater than you are able to bear, "trust in God and complain with all meekness to the officer that is set of God to forbid such violence." Furious and impatient conduct do not reflect God's presence on your side. However, if you are an officer, "then thou must be good, kind and merciful; but not a milksop and negligent." And "to whom thou art a father thou must rule, and make obedient, and that with sharpness, if softness will not be heard, and so in all other offices."[3]

---

1. Hans Kurath and Sherman M. Kuhn, eds., *Middle English Dictionary*, 11 vols. (Ann Arbor: University of Michigan Press, 1952–75), 7:268–73.

2. *The Bible in English*, CD-ROM (Cambridge: Chadwyck-Healey, 1996).

3. G. E. Duffield, ed., *The Work of William Tyndale* (Appleford, Berkshire, England: The Sutton Courtney Press, 1964), 199–200.

Tyndale here shows his understanding of the passive and active character of the meek. That he speaks of a person in office indicates he is aware of the connotations of leadership the word possesses. This understanding of Matthew 5:5 informs his translation of Matthew 11:29: "Take my yoke on you & lerne of me / for I am meke & lowly in herte." From Tyndale the word "meek" passed into the King James translation of 1611 and into our modern translations of the Bible. From table 2, however, one can see that the word has almost disappeared from modern biblical translations. The present study calls for a reassessment.

Table 2

Version	Hebrew Scriptures		New Testament			
	Num. 12:3	Ps. 37:11	Matt. 5:5	Matt. 11:29	Matt. 21:5	1 Peter 3:4
Older Translations (pre-1950)						
Wycliffe 1395	mylde	mylde	mylde	mylde	meke	mylde
Tyndale	meke	n/a	meke	meke	meke	meke
King James	meek	meek	meek	meek	meek	meek
American Standard	meek	meek	meek	meek	meek	meek
Tanakh (Jewish Publication Society)	meek	humble	n/a	n/a	n/a	n/a
1950–1960s						
Revised Standard	meek	meek	meek	gentle	humble	gentle
New English	of . . . humility	humble	of a gentle spirit	gentle	in gentleness	gentle
Jerusalem	humble	humble	gentle	gentle	humble	sweet
Today's English	humble	humble	humble	gentle	humble	gentle
Modern Translations						
New International	humble	meek	meek	gentle	gentle	gentle
New King James	humble	meek	meek	gentle	lowly	gentle
New Revised Standard	humble	meek	meek	gentle	humble	gentle
New American Standard	humble	humble	gentle	gentle	gentle	gentle
Revised English	of . . . humility	humble	gentle	gentle	in gentleness	gentle
New Jerusalem	humble	poor	gentle	gentle	humble	gentle
New American Bible	meekest	meek	meek	meek	meek	gentle
Inclusive NRS	n/a	meek	meek	meek	humble	gentle
New JPS Tanakh	humble	lowly	n/a	n/a	n/a	n/a

BIBLIOGRAPHY

Aasgaard, Reidar. "Brotherhood in Plutarch and Paul: Its Role and Character." In *Constructing Early Christian Families,* ed. Halvor Moxnes. New York and London: Routledge, 1997.

Adkins, Arthur. *Merit and Responsibility: A Study in Greek Values.* Oxford: Clarendon, 1960.

Allison, Dale. *The New Moses: A Matthean Typology.* Minneapolis: Fortress, 1993.

Audet, Jean-Paul. *La Didachè: Instructions des Apôtres.* Paris: J. Gabalda, 1958.

Barclay, William. *The Gospel of Matthew.* 2 vols. Louisville: Westminster/ John Knox, 1975.

Bauer, Walter, Wilhelm Arndt, Fredrich Gingrich, and F. W. Danker, eds. *A Greek-English Lexicon of the New Testament and Other Early Christian Literature.* Chicago: Chicago University Press, 1979.

Betz, Hans-Dieter. "The *Logion* of the Easy Yoke and of Rest." *Journal of Biblical Literature* 86 (1967): 10–24.

———. *The Sermon on the Mount.* Hermeneia. Minneapolis: Augsburg Fortress, 1995.

Betz, Hans-Dieter, and John M. Dillon. "*De cohibenda ira (Moralia* 452E– 46D)." In *Plutarch's Ethical Writings,* ed. Hans-Dieter Betz. Studia ad Corpus Hellenisticum Novi Testamenti 4. Leiden: Brill, 1978.

The Bible in English. CD-ROM. Cambridge: Chadwyck-Healey, 1996.

Bilde, Per, Troels Engberg-Pedersen, Lise Hannestad, and Jan Zahle, eds. *Aspects of Hellenistic Kingship.* Studies in Hellenistic Civilization 7. Oakville, Conn.: Aarhus University Press; Cambridge: Cambridge University Press, 1996.

Boring, M. Eugene. "The Gospel of Matthew." In *The New Interpreter's Bible.* 12 vols. Vol. 8. Nashville: Abingdon, 1995.

Bringmann, Klaus. "The King as Benefactor: Some Remarks on Ideal Kingship in the Age of Hellenism." In *Images and Ideologies: Self-Definition in the Hellenistic World,* ed. Anthony Bullock, Erich S.

Gruen, A. A. Long, and Andrew Stewart. Berkeley: University of California Press, 1993.

Budge, E. A. Wallis, ed. and trans. *Encomium of Theodosius, Archbishop of Alexandria, on Saint Michael the Archangel*. In *Miscellaneous Coptic Texts in the Dialect of Upper Egypt*. Reprint edition. New York: AMS Press, 1977.

Carter, Warren. *Households and Discipleship: A Study of Matthew 19–20*. Sheffield: Sheffield Academic Press, 1994.

Christie, Douglas Burton. *The Word in the Desert: Scripture and the Quest for Holiness in Early Christian Monasticism*. New York: Oxford University Press, 1983.

Collins, John J. *The Scepter and the Star: The Messiahs of the Dead Sea Scrolls and Other Ancient Literature*. New York: Doubleday, 1995.

Davies, W. D., and Dale C. Allison. *A Critical and Exegetical Commentary on the Gospel According to Saint Matthew*. 3 vols. Edinburgh: T. & T. Clark, 1988–1997.

Deutsch, Celia. *Hidden Wisdom and the Easy Yoke: Wisdom, Torah, and Discipleship in Matthew 11:25–30*. Sheffield: Sheffield Academic Press, 1987.

———. "Jesus-Wisdom the Teacher." In *Lady Wisdom, Jesus, and the Sages: Metaphor and Social Context in Matthew's Gospel*. Valley Forge, Pa.: Trinity Press International, 1996.

Du Bose, William Porcher. *The Gospel in the Gospels*. London: Longmans, Green and Co., 1906.

Duffield, G. E., ed. *The Work of William Tyndale*. Appleford, Berkshire, England: The Sutton Courtney Press, 1964.

Ehrenberg, Victor. *The Greek State*. 2d ed. Oxford: Basil Blackwell, 1969.

Ephippos in Athenaios. *Table Talk (Athenai Deipnosophistarum)*. Ed. G. Kaibel. Leipzig: Teubner, 1908.

Farrer, John. *Sermons on the Mission and Character of Christ, and on the Beatitudes*. Oxford: Oxford University, 1804.

Forbes, C. "Comparison, Self-Praise, and Irony in Paul's Boasting and the Conventions of Hellenistic Rhetoric." *New Testament Studies* 32 (1986): 1–30.

Foucault, Michel. *The History of Sexuality*. 3 vols. New York: Vintage, 1985.

Galen. *On the Natural Faculties*. Loeb Classical Library 71. Trans. Arthur John Brock. Cambridge, Mass.: Harvard University Press, 1916; rpr. 1991.

Good, Deirdre J. "The Verb ANACHŌREŌ, to Withdraw, in Matthew's Gospel." *Novum Testamentum* 32/1 (1990): 1–12.

Gore, Charles. *The Sermon on the Mount*. London: John Murray, 1896.

Gregory of Nyssa. *Gregorii Nysseni, de Oratione Dominica; de Beatitudinibus.* Edited and with a preface by Johannes F. Callahan. Leiden and New York: Brill, 1992.

Gruen, Erich S. "Fact and Fiction: Jewish Legends in a Hellenistic Context." In *Hellenistic Constructs: Essays in Culture, History, and Historiography,* ed. Peter Cartledge, Peter Garnsey, and Eric S. Gruen. Berkeley: University of California Press, 1997.

Guy, Jean-Claude. *Recherches sur la tradition grecque des Apophthegmata Patrum.* Subsidia Hagiographica 36. Brussels: Société de Bollandistes, 1962.

Halperin, David M., J. J. Winkler, and F. I. Zeitlin, eds. *Before Sexuality: The Construction of Erotic Experience in the Ancient Greek World.* Princeton: Princeton University Press, 1990.

Hartman, Joan E., and Ellen Messer-Davidow, eds. *(En)Gendering Knowledge: Feminists in Academe.* Knoxville: University of Tennessee Press, 1991.

Herman, Gabriel. "The Court Society of the Hellenistic Age." In *Hellenistic Constructs: Essays in Culture, History, and Historiography,* ed. Peter Cartledge, Peter Garnsey, and Eric S. Gruen. Berkeley: University of California Press, 1997.

Koester, Helmut. "Introduction to the Gospel According to Thomas." In *Nag Hammadi Codex II,2–7, Vol. 1.* Nag Hammadi Studies 20. Ed. Bentley Layton. Leiden: Brill, 1989.

Kurath, Hans, and Sherman M. Kuhn, eds. *Middle English Dictionary.* 11 vols. Ann Arbor: University of Michigan Press, 1952–1975.

Lake, Kirsopp, ed. and trans. *The Apostolic Fathers.* Loeb Classical Library. Cambridge, Mass: Harvard University Press, 1959.

Leivestad, Ragnar. " 'The Meekness and Gentleness of Christ': II Cor X,1." *New Testament Studies* 12–13 (1966): 156–64.

Lightfoot, J. B. *The Apostolic Fathers: English and Greek.* 3 vols. London: Macmillan, 1885.

Louw, Johannes P., and Eugene A. Nida, eds. *Greek-English Lexicon of the New Testament Based on Semantic Domains.* 2 vols. New York: United Bible Societies, 1988.

Luz, Ulrich. *Matthew 1–7: A Commentary.* Minneapolis: Augsburg, 1989.

Malherbe, Abraham. *Paul and the Thessalonians.* Philadelphia: Fortress, 1987.

Martin, Hubert, Jr. "The Concept of *Praotēs* in Plutarch's *Lives.*" *Greek, Roman, and Byzantine Studies* 3 (1960): 65–73.

Martínez, Florentino García, ed. and trans. *The Dead Sea Scrolls Translated: The Qumran Texts in English.* 2d ed. Leiden: Brill; Grand Rapids, Mich.: Eerdmans, 1996.

Meecham, H. G. *The Epistle to Diognetus.* Manchester: Manchester University Press, 1949.

Meeks, Wayne A. *The First Urban Christians: The Social World of the Apostle Paul.* New Haven, Conn.: Yale University Press, 1983.

Meyer, Marvin, ed. and trans. *The Gospel of Thomas.* San Francisco: HarperSanFrancisco, 1992.

Millar, Fergus. *The Roman Near East: 31 B.C.–A.D. 337.* Cambridge, Mass.: Harvard University Press, 1993.

Moore, Stephen D., and Janice Capel Anderson. "Taking It Like a Man: Masculinity in 4 Maccabees." *Journal of Biblical Literature* 117/2 (1998): 249–73.

Nielsen, Inge. *Hellenistic Palaces: Tradition and Renewal.* Studies in Hellenistic Civilization 5. Aarhus: Aarhus University Press, 1994.

The Oxford English Dictionary (Second Edition) on Compact Disc. Oxford: Oxford University Press, 1992.

Patte, Daniel. *The Gospel according to Matthew: A Structural Commentary on Matthew's Faith.* Philadelphia: Fortress, 1987; Valley Forge, Pa.: Trinity Press International, 1996.

Peters, F. E. *The Harvest of Hellenism: A History of the Near East from Alexander the Great to the Triumph of Christianity.* New York: Touchstone, Simon and Schuster, 1970.

Philo. *Moses.* Trans. F. H. Colson. In *Philo* 4. Loeb Classical Library. Cambridge, Mass.: Harvard University Press, 1966.

Pilch, John J., and Bruce J. Malina, eds. *Biblical Social Values and Their Meanings: A Handbook.* Peabody, Mass.: Hendrickson, 1993.

Rajak, Tessa. "Hasmonean Kingship and the Invention of Tradition." In *Aspects of Hellenistic Kingship,* ed. Per Bilde, Troels Engberg-Pedersen, Lise Hannestad, and Jan Zahle. Oakville, Conn.: Aarhus University Press, 1996.

de Romilly, Jacqueline. *La douceur dans la pensée grecque.* Paris: Société d'Édition, "Les Belles Lettres," 1979.

Rosenbaum, M., and A. M. Silbermann, eds. *Pentateuch with Targum Onkelos, Haphtaroth, and Rashi's Commentary.* 5 vols. Vol. 1. London: Shapiro, Vallentine, 1929.

Saldarini, A. J. *Pharisees, Scribes, and Sadducees in Palestinian Society: A Sociological Approach.* Wilmington, Del.: Glazier, 1988.

Sanday, William. *The Life of Christ in Recent Research.* New York: Oxford University Press, 1907.

Schmidt, Carl, ed. *Pistis Sophia.* Trans. Violet MacDermot. Nag Hammadi Studies 9. Leiden: Brill, 1978.

Schoedel, William R. *Ignatius of Antioch: A Commentary on the Letters of Ignatius of Antioch.* Hermeneia. Philadelphia: Fortress, 1985.

Schowalter, Dan. "Written in Stone: A Prayer to Augustus." In *Prayer from Alexander to Constantine: A Critical Anthology*, ed. Mark Kiley. London and New York: Routledge, 1997.

Scott, James C. *Domination and the Arts of Resistance*. New Haven, Conn., and London: Yale University Press, 1990.

Sim, David C. *Apocalyptic Eschatology in the Gospel of Matthew*. Cambridge: Cambridge University Press, 1996.

Smith, R. R. R. *Hellenistic Sculpture*. London: Thames and Hudson, 1991.

Soranus. *Gynecology*. Trans. O. Temkin. Baltimore and London: Johns Hopkins University Press, 1956.

Stanton, Graham. "Matthew 11:28–30: Comfortable Words?" In *A Gospel for a New People: Studies in Matthew*. Edinburgh: T. & T. Clark, 1992.

Stewart, Andrew. *Faces of Power: Alexander's Image and Hellenistic Politics*. Berkeley and Los Angeles: University of California Press, 1993.

Suggs, M. J. *Wisdom, Christology, and Law in Matthew's Gospel*. Cambridge, Mass.: Harvard University Press, 1970.

Tcherikover, Victor. *Hellenistic Civilization and the Jews*. Trans. S. Applebaum. New York: Athenaeum, 1970.

Vermes, Geza, ed. and trans. *The Complete Dead Sea Scrolls in English*. London and New York: Penguin, 1997.

Waddell, Helen. *The Desert Fathers*. London: Constable, 1936.

Walbank, F. W. "Monarchies and Monarchic Ideas." In *The Cambridge Ancient History*, vol. 7, 1. Cambridge: Cambridge University Press, 1982.

INDEX OF
ANCIENT SOURCES

INDEX OF SUBJECTS
AND MODERN AUTHORS